**Proceedings of the 1978 Clinic
on Library Applications
of Data Processing**

Papers presented at the
1978 Clinic on Library Applications
of Data Processing, April 23–26, 1978

Problems and Failures in Library Automation

F. WILFRID LANCASTER

Editor

University of Illinois
Graduate School of Library Science
Urbana-Champaign, Illinois

Clinic on Library Applications of Data Processing,
    University of Illinois at Urbana-Champaign, 1978.
    Problems and failures in library automation.

    (Proceedings of the 1978 Clinic on Library Applications of Data Processing)
    On spine: library applications of data processing, 1978.
    Includes index.
    1. Libraries—Automation—Congresses. 2. Library science—Data process-
ing—Congresses. I. Lancaster, Frederick Wilfrid. 1933–   II. Title. III. Title:
Library applications of data processing. 1978. IV. Series: Clinic on Library Applications of Data Processing. Proceedings; 1978.

Z678.9.A1C5   1978   025′.02′02854   78-31801
ISBN 0-87845-050-5

CONTENTS

INTRODUCTION

THE FIFTEENTH ANNUAL Clinic on Library Applications of Data Processing was held April 23–26, 1978, at the Illini Union Building, University of Illinois at Urbana-Champaign. At earlier clinics the papers were almost exclusively positive in their views of library automation. They reported successes rather than failures and benefits rather than problems. For the 1978 clinic, however, an attempt was made to find speakers willing to present the other side of the coin. The papers in the present volume, therefore, deal with problems—or, in some cases, downright failures—in the automation of various facets of library service. They range from Veaner's general survey of failures/limitations in library automation as a whole to case studies of failures or problems encountered in specific applications or environments. It is perhaps not too surprising to find that the most abject failures are attributable more to management ineptness and bureaucratic bungling than to inadequacies in existing technology. This volume is presented in the hope that the library profession can learn at least as much from its failures as it can from its successes.

F. WILFRID LANCASTER
Editor

ALLEN B. VEANER
University Librarian
University of California
Santa Barbara

What Hath Technology Wrought?*

I BELIEVE IT WAS Adali Stevenson who said: "Man does not live by words alone, but he sometimes has to eat them." No one wants to be reminded of anything but his successes! So, I sense that in putting together their papers for these proceedings, my colleagues have squirmed at least as uncomfortably as I. Librarians know that the inventory of failures in library automation is long and dismal. However, this is not intended to be a series of obituaries; rather, my purpose is to review the period of transition from completely manual to nearly fully automated systems, to try to see what can be learned from analyzing the failures, and to extract some general observations in answer to the question: what hath technology wrought?

It is written that the earth was formless and void in the beginning. The world of bibliography and library science, however, was far from chaotic twenty years ago when computers first began to make an impact beyond pure science. In fact, the theory, methods and procedures of bibliography were well defined and clearly articulated, if admittedly imperfect. What has sent the field reeling in the past two decades is not the computer but the worldwide social changes leading to enormously increased publication output and service expectations far beyond those we

*I acknowledge the assistance and advice of the following persons who kindly agreed to review the penultimate draft of the manuscript and offer critical suggestions and comments: Richard De Gennaro, Richard M. Dougherty, Karen Horny, Susan K. Martin, Stephen R. Salmon, and David C. Weber.

had been prepared to meet in the past. If we can fly from New York to London in three and one-half hours, send people to the moon, print thousands of lines of text per minute, obtain a fully developed color picture in a minute or two, and take instant movies, why must it take months or years to acquire, catalog and put into the hand of users a variety of library materials? Surely technology could help solve such a seemingly simple problem.

Before a problem can be solved, however, it must be defined. In this area the library profession was inexperienced and ill-prepared. Into this atmosphere, composed of equal portions of good intentions and ignorance, came three forces: "computerniks" with little exposure to libraries, librarians with little experience in defining problems quantitatively, and federal money. When the protective amulet of outside fiscal sponsorship is available, it is a fact that it becomes difficult to refrain from going forth either to explore regions unknown, to heal the sick or to bring the faith to unbelievers. There was no shortage of unbelievers.

A popular cliché has it that many modern problems stem from the difference between the paces of technological and social development. Systems change by months or years, people by lifetimes, and with so many contemporary generations out of phase with technological development, conflict is inevitable. It is easy to look at the broad picture historically and exculpate ourselves for failures of library automation by pointing to the forces larger than ourselves, to the circumstances of which we are the victims. It is quite another thing to take individual responsibility and see how we may have contributed separately and collectively to those larger forces.

Word v. Deed

One immediate failure, or human frailty perhaps, was the confounding of word and deed, of concept and reality; or less obliquely, of the promised schedule and the actual schedule. Fifteen years ago I recall hearing Calvin Mooers say why there were so few truly operational information systems. He ascribed this lack to the simple ability of people to distinguish work from fun. Designing information systems was fun; making them operate was work. Some people are interested in intellectual challenge as a game, others want to create production systems to perform work. When these two types cooperate on the same project, disaster is bound to ensue.

The Immodest and the Modest

Although conventional wisdom would have us all be self-effacing, there are some good words to be said about the immodest people who began to shake up this profession. It takes a lot of nerve and substantial self-confidence to be an upstart, to try to crack the traditional structure of a naturally conservative establishment—and until recently, systems of bibliographic control changed at an undeniably glacial pace. These immodest people possess vision and a powerful imagination; they are a creative force. Immodesty, like many creative qualities, has a double edge. Its second perspective is the deplorable mixture of elitism and naïveté which initially afflicted some librarians and computer experts alike. Talk was cheap, slick and glib. One pioneer in library automation was heard to say: "To the arm-wavers goes the credit." While assigning to hapless but talented programmers the pleasures of staying up all night to write code, test and debug programs, the self-promoters made hay in the sunshine. Many of the talkers wore the emperor's clothes; some designers liked to play God. They were sure they could tell librarians what was good for the library even though they didn't make much use of libraries themselves.

Lack of Direction from the Profession

For a long time the library profession permitted the technological tail to wag the bibliographic dog. This lack of direction from top management may have been the most serious of all our failures. It led to tremendous waste of financial and human resources. But let us not blame the technicians. They came from mission-oriented environments where the rewards go to the strong. Most librarians came from educational backgrounds lacking strength in management science and technology. Thus, it is no wonder that technicians, sensing a lack of authority, ran amok, setting their own goals and priorities. The worst cases ended in utter failure. Most came out in the middle with powerful strengths and enervating weaknesses side by side, and by the mid-1970s, none even approached the system features and facilities forecast a decade earlier.

After these excesses of the 1960s and early 1970s, I hope that the library profession will exert its leadership and never again permit technology to become the driving force in system development. To employ an anology from air transportation, we permit designers and engineers to test and build aircraft, but responsibility for determination of routes, hiring of pilots and marketing of an airlines service is assigned to management and not delegated to technicians. It is recognized that in the early stages of any technological development, the technical and managerial functions are commonly combined in one person or a small cadre. As a field matures, however, technical and managerial aspects inevitably split and are assigned to persons with different talents. In library automation too, this division should occur as the field matures. In this way we will be certain that technology will always be the servant, never the master.

Failure to Achieve Cost Advantage

We grossly underestimated the cost-effectiveness of some manual library systems. With automation we have still failed to realize significant staff savings (especially in cataloging), and more remarkably, we have—with one or two notable exceptions—ignored the much greater potential for savings in acquisitions where the transaction volume is five to ten times greater than in cataloging. Acquisitions require that we search, order, receive, cancel, claim, pay, post vendor reports, and execute a host of other purchase-related transactions, meaning that the total activity is far greater than that in cataloging.

We probably have been further seduced by the falsehood that falling unit costs in computers would save us from rising personnel costs. It is true that the falling unit cost of computer hardware is one component of saving. Unfortunately, as computers and systems become more sophisticated, they require an ever-increasing staff of highly sophisticated and expensive software people for maintenance and development. The rise of this personnel component of the computer far offsets any personnel savings in actual library operations. Ignoring the self-generating character of automated systems has further contributed to the failure to achieve cost savings: success breeds accelerated use. Increased use costs more money, so the bottom line is bigger. An automated system is always required to do more than the manual system it replaced; it is this "doing more" which costs more.

To some extent we also have been attracted by the appealing argument of "around-the-corner-ism." By this I mean the promise of tomorrow's technology—whether it be in the form of satellite transmission of data, distributed computing, higher storage densities, or the like. It has led us to believe that technological advances will continue the downward spiral of costs. For every decline in hardware costs, there appears to be a correspondingly greater increase in the cost of the staff required to support that hardware, a point alluded to above.

Failure to Achieve Simplicity

We have not succeeded in making life simpler, easier and cheaper for ourselves. We have designed rigid, deterministic styles of interaction with the computer—a far cry from Licklider's procognitive system.[1] Highly restrictive protocols for person/machine communication impose huge training loads and require massive amounts of documentation, which is often neither well written nor of sufficient quantity or depth. Yet another consequence has been across-the-board reclassification of operating personnel with greater total personnel cost resulting even when the staff is reduced. The bottom line has become larger, not smaller.

In asking, "What do you want?" during the development of MARC, we may have been asking the wrong question. The predictable response, "We want everything," may have led directly to the complexity and expense we now face in handling MARC, a format which continues to grow in theological complexity. In the developmental stages, no one appears to have asked these three questions: (1) What do we need in a machine-readable bibliographic format? (2) Why do we need it? (3) How much can we afford to pay for it? Had these questions been answered, we might have had a quite different and less elaborate MARC. These same questions naturally apply to the entire system design process.

I have always felt strongly that we needed one or more standard subsets of the MARC format, subsets selected for a variety of purposes. This might have saved the expense and complexity of processing the full MARC format for simpler applications and would also have encouraged local input in accordance with national standards. While serving on the RECON Working Task Force, I urged adoption of a simple, fundamental subset of MARC for converting retrospective records, a subset which could be upgraded on demand. It seemed that given a defined subset, RECON might have been achieved at costs considerably below the then-estimated $10 million. Although at the time librarians in this country were not ready to agree on a standard subset, our Canadian colleagues successfully defined and implemented a mini-MARC format. It seems ironic that while we have worried so much about exponential growth of our collections and their appetite for dollars and space, we have been oblivious to the ever-escalating costs of data input and conversion for titles having very little potential for actual use or access. Why waste money inputting records in full MARC format when there is little or no evidence of demand? The mini-MARC or subset idea would at least permit minimal access to the total bibliographic record and later, appropriate data management systems could tell us which records are vital and worthy of update to full MARC. Massive conversion to the full format, however, does not appear to be economically justifiable.

The Bibliographic Balance of Payments—A Failure in Pricing

We have failed to develop satisfactory price alogrithms. In the case of OCLC, the price algorithm stimulated a proliferation of similar entries into the data base by those shortsighted persons who wished to evade a first time use charge. In the case of BALLOTS, there was a bewildering mixture of charges for telecommunications, connect time and batch outputs. In the end we seemed so caught up in the novel aspects of the computer that we didn't wish to recognize the simple fact that resources are finite, that computer transactions—like people transactions—cost money. Some balked at the notion of paying for a service. The idea that one ever pays for anything related to an information service seems an anathema to a good many librarians and is guaranteed to elicit an emotional response. We pay for books but want our cataloging and access for free. In this connection we will face continuing challenges from the commercial sector which is working very hard to deliver information and data, while libraries and library networks are still delivering citations.

We have indulged in a good deal of talk about shared cataloging and enjoyed some limited implementation—but no network has yet succeeded in establishing an equitable arrangement for a supplier/benefactor relationship which parallels the emerging charge system for interlibrary loans. Just as the largest research libraries can no longer continue to subsidize interlibary loan for the have-not libraries, neither can they continue to input expensive original cataloging into a data base only to have other libraries obtain a free ride on it. Somehow the balance of bibliographic payments has to be realized, and I see this as a major future challenge for all networks.

Scheduling Problems: Slippage

As with many computer projects in other fields, we have demonstrated a total inability to get anything done on schedule. This failure is partly attributable to traditional underestimation of task difficulty and partly attributable to poor management. In the latter area, our inexperience in system design has kept us from understanding the reality that by a given date every system must be closed to all further design change. That means, of course, that the analysis upon which the new design is based must be as complete as possible; something important that has been overlooked until programming is well underway naturally has a harmful effect on the schedule.

Aside from insufficient analysis, overcommitment of resources has been a troublesome contributor to late delivery. Some people believe that it is always possible to take on one more task, to add one more "goodie" to the design. It's possible, yes, but it's not possible to do this and also maintain a schedule.

Designing and programming are activities quite different from digging ditches or hauling freight, where more can get done by adding more diggers or trucks. That this can be done with intellectual work is a terrible misconception! Some have learned the hard way that adding staff does not accelerate schedules. In fact, it has exactly the opposite effect, because it introduces additional managerial and internal communication complexities. Frederick Brooks, Jr., author of *The Mythical Man-Month,* has expressed this phenomenon succinctly and accurately: adding staff to a late software project makes it later.[2]

Scheduling Problems: Sequencing

Although we recognized that the name authority problem had to be solved in order to manage massive bibliographic files, we worked first on a format for the dissemination of bibliographic data. From the hindsight of today's knowledge, this sequence was undoubtedly wrong, and it is interesting to speculate how the MARC format might look today if the authority contol problem had been addressed first.

Lack of Perspective

In a period of rapid development it is common to confound a first-generation system with the ultimate. Yet we may have allowed a kind of parental pride to foster emotional loyalties to our creations, loyalties which beclouded perceptions and permitted us to ignore obvious limitations or disadvantages. We have handled these newborn systems as if they were personalities rather than mere tools to exploit. The history of technology demonstrates conclusively that the first system or device in any development is crude and unsophisticated, no matter how wondrous it may appear to its early users. The Wright Flyer is not the Boeing 747. Today's hand-held minicomputers rival or surpass the power of the first electronic computers which took up a whole roomful of space and consumed tons of air conditioning. Today $400 can buy a palm-sized television set that weighs twenty-six ounces. Perhaps librarianship may be forgiven for its initial, overenthusiastic response to its first automated tools. After all, except for typewriters and telephones, there hasn't been much mechanical aid in librarianship. And we have only enjoyed comparatively inexpensive photocopying within the past twenty years. Perhaps it is too much to expect a parent to cast a cold eye on his or her offspring. But isn't it time now to take a dispassionate and objective look at our systems?

Looking Backward Instead of Forward

We continue to build great computerized bibliographic empires based on the tottering foundations of aging control systems and antiquated concepts. Our systems are conceived and organized conservatively—they have to be, because their purpose is to maintain the established order. Our designs are largely retrospective, based as they are on the ideas of continuity and integrity of the bibliographic control apparatus. These noble concepts are admirable, but I wonder if they have become sacred cows! Where are the users and the patrons in all of this? Users are interested in obtaining library materials; they show little interest in the niceties of elegant bibliographic superstructures.

The computer is a totally new and revolutionary tool for bibliographic control and access. It threatens an established bureaucracy. We have tried to graft it to existing library procedures and methods. The card catalog is an example. What has driven us to consider closing our card catalogs is not the computer's potential, but ever-increasing labor costs. Most of our systems, however, have been geared to using the computer as a giant, fast card-printer. In his *Annual Review of Information Science and Technology* article on on-line systems, Davis McCarn says: "We still remain disconcertingly far from closing the card catalog. . . . Even more disconcerting is the lack of thought on how to take advantage of the new computer technology."[3] He goes on to complain that we have not used imagination in applying the computer to subject access, agreeing with Bates that the profession has taken as a given the structure of the card catalog with its impoverished approach to topical retrieval.[4] Commander Edward Whitehead, the distinguished British marketing representative of Schweppes Ltd., has formulated a dictum which might be observed as profitably in the library profession as in the beverage business: "Excessive virtue is as difficult to sustain as none at all. . . . Perfection tries the patience of one's family and friends"[5]—and I might add: of one's professional colleagues. I have maintained elsewhere that perfectionism is a sickness of librarianship. It is as if the penalty for spoiling a bibliographic record were to be shot at sunrise. Our continuing preoccupation—one is almost inclined to say mania—with the cosmetic aspects of card production may be further proof of the myopia of perfectionism. It seems ironic that this preoccupation continues in the face of certain closure of card catalogs within a decade or so. Is this another demonstration of the profession's confusion of appearance and substance, a failure to distinguish between the medium and the message? We seem to forget that the public prefers library materials to good-looking catalog cards. I hope the demise of the card catalog will redirect the attention of the profession toward the real information needs of our clientele.

We might profitably ask another basic question about our approach to bibliographic access. Have we failed to distinguish a document from its surrogate, library materials from their bibliographic records? Early in the application of mechanical accounting machines to librarianship, we bewailed the fact that these machines could print only uppercase letters. Once we had acquired advanced machines to print upper- and lowercase letters, we bemoaned the fact that we could not represent diacritical marks and special characters. Now that we have that capability, we complain that they are not displayed in the correct position on the CRT. Yet no investigation has ever been undertaken to determine the essentiality of such luxuries to the purpose for which the catalog exists, nor has anyone analyzed the incremental cost of providing these extra features and whether we could afford these increments or not. It is an incontrovertible fact that the library market is too small and insignificant to stimulate major equipment manufacturers on their own to produce the highly complex graphic character representations we would *like* to have but for which proof of need has never been given. Only when the industry at large perceives a condition of readiness in the market beyond librarianship is the point reached at which an aggressive response is forthcoming, one from which the library profession can benefit. Instead of being grateful for a new but limited capability, however, our attitude has often been that "if we can't have everything, then we don't want anything." This attitude may be linked to the tradition of perfectionism in librarianship and to cosmetic rather than substantive aspects of performance. For a service-oriented organization it is an attitude that is neither healthy nor realistic, and I hope it will soon change.

Concept of Development Imperfectly Understood

Development is a comparatively new concept in the library profession. There wasn't much of it prior to the computer and what there was occurred at such a slow pace that it was imperceptible to most librarians. Unlike Spinozistic ethics or biological growth, development is not a deterministic process, yet some people expected library automation systems to hatch fully formed, the way a butterfly emerges from a chrysalis. Few will disagree today that library automation simply *has* to be one of the most complex and challenging professional assignments of the century. We also know that highly complex processes develop comparatively slowly, at about the same pace as human growth. We librarians sometimes take for granted the depth, complexity, magnitude and sophistication of what we do in libraries. From time to time we ought to remind ourselves that we deal with every script, every language, every period of history, every intellectual discipline, every country, every region, innumerable forms of material, and a time span exceeding half a milennium for printed materials (and well beyond that for manuscripts)—an incredible array of human communication media covering an almost unlimited time span. The integration of this into computer procedures invokes a technology that cannot be implemented in a fortnight. If my contention that computerized bibliographic systems mature at the same pace as human beings is accepted, then our on-line production systems are operating at about the level of an eight-year-old child. As we do not expect eight-year-olds to behave as if they were mature adults, we should likewise cultivate patience and enjoy one of the great pleasures of parenthood—watching a being grow and develop. At the same time, we had better behave like responsible parents and not believe that our child can do no wrong. A 1967 report on computers in higher education begins by stating: "After growing wildly for years, the field of computing now appears to be approaching its infancy."[6] Library computing is now well past infancy and is approaching a sturdy adolescence. But let's not delude outselves into thinking it has reached maturity. We have a long way to go.

Has Our Conceptual Scale Been Too Grandiose?

Almost eighty-five years ago, there was founded in Brussels the International Institute of Bibliography, an organization dedicated to the idea of universal bibliographic control through the then comparatively novel card catalog. By 1911, sixteen years after the institute was founded, its master catalog contained 8 million cards, copies of which could be ordered for 10 *centimes* each. The mission of the institute was no less ambitious than worldwide bibliographic control. Fortunately for this country, the Library of Congress's card printing program was much less ambitious, and perhaps thereby more practical and durable. The Brussels institute may be an early example of technology's reach exceeding its grasp. Had the world remained steady-state, there might have been hope. But as this favorable condition never exists, we always ought to recognize that systems, like people have definite lifetimes; new problems arise to which the old systems can no longer be responsive. Only a new system can help in such cases. Eventually, that new system becomes unresponsive, dies and is replaced. Bibliographic systems are merely mortal. If the International Institute of Bibliography could not succeed in controlling the pre-World War I literature, and if the Library of Congress recognized the limitations of its own control system, why do we continue so audaciously to believe that we with our computers now have the power to control the millions of new titles with their tens and hundreds of millions of access points, all emanating from hundreds of countries and thousands of jurisdictions? Are we demonstrating some colossal gall, some unjustifiable *chutzpah*? Do we really know enough to take on the universe? Assuming we do know enough, what makes us so sure that society will finance such massive systems? The time may have come for us to consider scaling down our goals to more realistic enterprises. Like NASA, should we reach for the moon and some of the planets instead of the stars?

In an address prepared for last year's conference of the American Association for the Advancement of Science, Dr. Lewis Thomas, author of *The Lives of a Cell,* said:

> These are not the best times for the human mind. All sorts of
> things seem to be turning out wrong, and the century seems to be

slipping through our fingers here at the end, with almost all promises unfilled. . . . Just think, two centuries ago we could explain everything about everything, out of pure reason, and now most of that elaborate and harmonious structure has come apart before our eyes. We are *dumb*.[7]

One way of getting smarter is perhaps to scale down our goals and expectations to a more realistic level. In this connection I may cite the extraordinarily difficult design challenge faced by Japanese software designers in attempting to build a completely automated hot standby dual processor for a nationwide bank control system. The designers hoped to develop a system in which one processor would take over instantaneously when the other went down. The design chief reports: "As the system design work progressed, however, we found that software development was a lot more difficult and complex than anticipated. Therefore we lowered our objectives to a more realistic level."[8]

One of the things to think about is the comparative isolation of bibliographic systems from society at large. Until recently I think it fair to say that, bibliographically speaking, many of the librarians and faculty in academe really resided in a walled medieval city, living out a manorial economy of self-sufficiency in collection development and technical processing. Meanwhile, a money and mercantile economy was growing because of improved roads and vehicles. In modern terms, the walled cities begin to lose their walls when a communication network develops to the point where commerce and exchange becomes a more vital social force than self-sufficiency. That is where I believe we are today in our biblioeconomy. The walls are tumbling down. Our technology is reaching the point where the vision of the nation's libraries as a single, national bibliographic resource can be realized, but only if we can sell the idea to the funders. This is the vision which the National Commission on Libraries and Information Science is trying to promote. It is a vision many of us may see turned into reality in our lifetimes, a reality built upon both our failures and our achievements.

Janet Flanner, the well-known writer for *The New Yorker,* at the age of eighty-six recently stated: "Nothing is improved by chance. Nothing grows better by error. Everything always grows better because someone says: 'I can't stand this any longer!' "[9] A counterpart of such a statement in library systems development might be: "This no longer works," or "We can't afford this solution any longer." The massive union catalog projects of the 1920s and 1930s are an example. These were, after all, not new technological solutions but merely the continuation of the concept begun three-quarters of a century ago by the International Institute of Bibliography. We gave up those concepts because they had become dysfunctional. We ought to ask of our current enthusiasms: "What elements of dysfunction are embryonic within them?" In my opinion a major component of the response is *overcomplexity,* fueled by funds, ambitions, distorted perspectives, and perhaps even misplacement of priorities. Yet a mistake is not a tragedy. We should not berate the past for our mistakes, but rather build constructively upon them. After all, we do not fault the baby who stumbles while learning to walk. The mistakes of the past must be used for construction and reconstruction, and not for pinning the blame on any one person or institution.

Will we face again the mistakes of the past—lack of humility and an overbearing sense of self-importance? We talk as if automated bibliography were one of the most important things in the world. Yet the world goes on without it, thriving. Most citizens have no concept of bibliographic control and access systems and probably wouldn't care about them even if someone were to take the time and trouble to explain them. Yet we specialists want public funds to pay for the development and operation of large systems we claim will benefit all people. Thus, the challenge of the future remains where it has always been—not in technology per se, but in our human adaptation to it. When resources are limited, we have to sell librarianship and bibliography to the funding agencies. We have to convince them that our services are essential elements of public policy. Libraries can no longer survive just because dedicated professionals and some high-spirited citizens believe they are intrinsically "good." There are many other "good" things in the world competing for resources. Our future responses to social and technological challenge must not resemble what I have described in this paper.

A scenario I would like to see in librarianship should resemble that described by Yuzuru Abe, the designer responsible for the Japanese on-line banking system mentioned earlier: "This February, our new on-line system centered around three super-scale computers went into operation. . . . It took three years and 3200 man months [267 man years] to develop the . . . system. Currently, our terminal system consists of 700 minicomputers and 4000 terminals, all up and running. At the time of this writing, we were in our 150th day of continuous service without downtime."[10] This level of operation represents an exceedingly high standard worthy of emulation.

I would prefer to title some future review "What Have *We* Wrought?" in the hope that some day, we'll be wise enough to have exercised adequate professional leadership—which will not only assure our survival but also guarantee that we survive as the masters of technology, not as its slaves.

REFERENCES

1. Licklider, J.C. *Libraries of the Future*. Cambridge. MIT Press, 1965.

2. Brooks, Frederick P., Jr. "The Mythical Man-Month," *Datamation* 20:48, Dec. 1974. *See also*_____. *The Mythical Man-Month: Essays on Software Engineering*. Reading, Mass., Addison-Wesley, 1974.

3. McCarn, Davis B. "On-line Systems—Techniques & Services." *In* Martha E. Williams ed. *Annual Review of Information Science and Technology, Vol. 13*. White Plains, N.Y., Knowledge Industry Publications, Inc., p. 93.

4. Bates, Marcia J. "Factors Affecting Subject Catalog Search Success," *JASIS* 28:161–69, May 1977.

5. Whitehead, Edward. "The Commander's Regime," *Mainliner* 22:40, April 1978.

6. President's Science Advisory Committee. *Computers in Higher Education*. Washington, D.C., USGPO, 1967, p. 1.

7. Thomas, Lewis. Quoted *in* Jeremy Bernstein. "Biology Watcher," *The New Yorker* 53:45–46, Jan. 2, 1978.

8. Abe, Yuzuru. "A Japanese On-Line Banking System," *Datamation* 23:97, Sept. 1977.

9. Flanner, Janet. " 'The Originals' Debuts on KCET," *The Los Angeles Times,* April 15, 1978, p. B9, col. 2.

10. Abe, op. cit., p. 89.

ESTELLE BRODMAN
Librarian and Professor of Medical History
School of Medicine
Washington University
St. Louis, Missouri

Reactions to Failures
in Library Automation

IN 1968 AND 1969 Doris Bolef, Lynda Van Wagoner and I published two articles reporting the failure of a computer-based cataloging system which we had developed for the Washington University School of Medicine Library in St. Louis.[1] These articles discussed the theory behind our system, the methods and programs used, and the unsatisfactory results, and announced that we were scrapping the old system and starting all over to design an entirely new one. We also examined the reasons we could adduce for the lack of success and made a few tentative remarks about the lessons we had learned from our failure.

Surprisingly, these seemingly innocuous papers brought forth a spate of letters—to us and to the editors of various journals[2]—which stated that at best we were incompetent bumblers and that at worst we were heretics who had betrayed the godhead, the teachings from "on high," and the faith we were sworn to uphold. I finally replied in one publication: "Forgive me if I seem weary of this argument. Since I have had to write several letters like this, I am sending a copy to the Editor of *Special Libraries* and asking him to print it."[3]

Since then I have not published any other articles which report a failure in automation in quite so much detail, so I do not know if the severity and tone of attack on authors who do report such situations is still as great as it was eight or nine years ago. However, according to a recent article in *SLJ Hotline*[4] and to Steve Salmon's article in *The Information Age,* only a small number of failures in library automation have been reported; Salmon states that the literature on the failures suggests that: "Those experiments which did not work were considered failures. . . . The real failure of most of these projects is the lack of reporting . . . on . . . them."[5] Several years ago Bruer noted that when there is a failure in automation, articles on it "decrease drastically until . . . almost nothing is reported in the literature."[6] Perhaps all this secrecy is like Walter Cronkite's feeling about negative news. Reporting negative news on the air, he once told an interviewer, is a little like writing a story about a cat that *didn't* get stuck in a tree. Also, the very normal human trait of not wishing to appear foolish, as well as the feeling of frustration when reality doesn't measure up to one's expectations, have much to do with the lack of negative reporting in the field.

Like Bergson, however, I believe there is no explanation, there are only explanations. I know of at least three other contributing reasons which might explain the dearth of reports telling of the demise or required reconstruction of library automation systems. These are: (1) the emotion of the newly-converted, (2) the attitude of librarians and others dealing with libraries concerning funds, and (3) the difficulty many librarians seem to have in understanding exactly what is subsumed under the words "research and development."

Varieties of Religious Experience

So common is the zeal of the newly-converted that proverbs have been formed in many languages to describe this folk knowledge. In French, converts are called more regal than the king; in Hebrew, more orthodox than the rabbi; and in American slang, more religious than God, or more Catholic than the pope. The reasons for this experience are not hard to find. The convert is looked upon with some suspicion by those who have been in the group for a long time; they question that the conversion was real, that the convert will not soon relapse into his old ways. To combat this suspicion, the new member of the clan must give greater assurance of his faith and faithfulness than is expected of one who has been tested by past experiences; small things which are of no concern to the accepted member become crucial for the new one. He dare not appear to have any doubts about the wisdom of his choice. Another reason is that a new convert lacks the experience to differentiate that which is fundamental to his new faith from that which is peripheral and comparatively unimportant. His usual answer to this dilemma is to treat everything as equally—and vitally—important. Both the belief in one God and the necessity of facing toward Mecca when praying are thus of the same importance to the new convert, but are usually placed in perspective by the Muslim of many years' standing.

Finally, the convert has probably come to his new position after conflicts with his former group, to whom he has usually proclaimed the superiority of his new religion. He may have been told by his old colleagues that he has been brainwashed or that he is betraying the group that nurtured him. Under these circumstances he feels he dare not go back to the old group, even if he finally comes to agree with them. The only answer is to continue to assert that the new belief is not less valuable than he had proclaimed previously. All arguments against the new creed must be overturned—by reason if possible, or by a call for faith if reason cannot prevail.

I think the relationship between these things and the feelings of many librarians about automation in the 1960s must be fairly obvious. Many of these librarians came to automation as new converts, often without being completely sure of the basis for library automation; some, indeed, came only after being pushed into it by their administrators. Automation, for them, *had* to be the truth and the way; they dared not even appear to lack adherence to either the major or the minor tenets of the faith, lest they themselves become suspect; and they could not let their erstwhile colleagues and friends think they had been foolishly brainwashed. Instead, they must turn on the questioner and demolish his arguments, somehow, for the good of the faith and the convert's peace of mind. The letters I received seem to me to be the expected result of such mixed feelings.

There is, however, another way of looking at the effects of conversion and sectarian heresies, and this is a more optimistic view. The very fact that heresies develop causes changes in established religions; every reformation has its equivalent counterreformation, in which the original creeds and the accepted institutional actions are examined and modified in light of this examination: thus Luther's Ninety-five Theses on the church door wiped out much of simony and the sale of indulgences in the Catholic church; Hahnemann's homeopathy did away with polypharmacy and enormous doses of drugs in eclectic medicine, as well as introduce the concept of the patient as an individual. Gradually, the original belief and the heresy become indistinguishable, as the best of both systems are molded into one, until finally it is difficult to tell them apart without a scorecard.

This is what has happened with library automation. Many of us can remember when there were two schools of thought about computers in libraries; when those who were opposed to it (whether because they felt threatened by it, or just couldn't stand the boasts and posturings of the newly-converted) would rejoice at the reports of computer foul-ups. Accounts of overpayments of checks, confused department store charge accounts, and the failures of bank vaults run by computers to open on time would be posted gleefully on library bulletin boards. A decade later, however, computer system developers have come to examine more soberly the complaints of the disgruntled and incorporated many of them into their work, and the unconvinced have had to add computers to their everyday lives, with the result that the sharp distinction between believers and heretics has almost been wiped out. I say "almost," because I still sense a tendency of some librarians to equate computers with black magic and their users with powerful spirits. An example is to be found among those librarians who search the many computerized data bases now available to answer inquiries and so consider themselves a group apart from the other librarians. The mystique of data base searches fascinates and amuses me, but I believe with time this too will pass.

Librarians as Churchmice

All that I have just said is only one portion of the picture. There are other reasons for the actions we saw, and one has to do with the psychological effects of poverty. Most libraries have traditionally been starved for the resources which would allow them to perform efficiently the tasks for which the library was originally established. The old joke is that librarians are mice in two senses: they squeak and run away and they are as poor as churchmice. Scott Adams said that after grants were set up through the Medical Library Assistance Act of 1965, librarians were so used to being poor that they didn't know how to use money when it did become available. Whether or not this is true, it certainly is true that when money is in short supply, the misuse of any of it becomes a sin—just as gluttony was a mortal sin in medieval times when food was scarce, but became unimportant as newer methods of agriculture provided everyone with fuller diets.

This is also compounded by the fact that society has accepted the librarians' views of resources for libraries. Most administrators, boards of trustees and university presidents expect that the library's funds will be spent carefully, frugally, with maximum return for the outlay, and without risk. Librarians are not expected to be innovators of untried systems for several reasons. They are too often thought to be intellectually or emotionally incapable of handling innovations (present company excepted, of course); moreover, if the money is spent unwisely, there are no backup funds to substitute for the lost resources. A library *must* succeed with its programs or make do without other programs.

If a librarian has spent much effort and time convincing budgeting officials to allow him to automate part of the library's work, there is great pressure to have that automation do all the good things he has assured the president or dean or board of trustees it will do. When it does not work, it must be patched up here and there to cover up the deficiencies of the system—rather than scrapped and begun all over again—in the hope that things will work out before the complaints of users reach that president or dean or trustee who was "brainwashed." At the very least, he will try to find in the failed system some unexpected benefits for the library, which will then be viewed and reported as successes. This is necessary not only because he fears a drop in status due to failure, not only because everyone will say, "I told you so," but because the librarian knows perfectly well that he has mortgaged his library account as well as his soul, and that there is no more of either when the devil's—or the computer sales representative's—system is a flop. He realizes it will compound his problems if the automation fails, for he will have as a result neither automation nor a good acquisitions or catalog program. He dare not start all over again; but even if he wanted to, he couldn't, because there are no additional funds available. Consequently, if someone else reports that the system fails, he feels the necessity to shut that person up or to downgrade him for his own safety. This is an old Ciceronian ploy—if you cannot find reasoned arguments against an opponent, call him names or imply nefarious motives. "Oh, Roman Senators," you thunder, "Oh, patres conscripti, is this not the man who was found in the vestal virgin's house on the night of the last Saturnalia?" even though you know perfectly well it wasn't this man at all, and even if it were, that has nothing to do with the case you are arguing. I fear that this was the unconscious reaction of some people to our articles; all I can say here is that we might have been stupid, but venal we were not. So far as I know, no member of my staff was ever found in the vestal virgin's house—on the night of the Saturnalia, or any other night!

Research and Development

Finally, there is the third possible explanation of the reaction to failure in automation mentioned earlier—misunderstanding of the terms *research* and *development*. Old and established disciplines tend to have an underpinning of sound knowledge of the fundamental laws of their fields. The laws of falling bodies, of immune response to infection, of drought and famine are well understood, and a whole series of actions can be built on this knowledge. We know why vaccination with cowpox will protect one against smallpox, and we can calculate how long it will take the lighted ball on top of the Times Building in New York's Times Square to reach the ground on New Year's Eve; and we act on this knowledge. In a new field, however, these fundamental laws are still unknown, and most research must be focused on uncovering them. This is the most arduous, most frustrating, but most exciting, fulfilling and rewarding part of research and development. Only when this work is done can the development part of research and development follow. The changes for success in research are, of course, always problematic, for if one knew for sure that something would be true, then acting on that knowledge would not be experimentation. Research is essentially answering two questions: what happens, and why does it happen? All else is window-dressing.

Even when the fundamental bases for a discipline are fairly certain, there is no end to the search for data and their explication. Not only does the uncovering of new data change what seemed at the time reasonable explanations of natural phenomena (for example, the switch from the corpuscular theory of light to the wave theory), but there still remain the problems of determining how the basic factors act and interact in different environments and under different conditions. This is the development side of research and development: the fleshing out of fundamental knowledge for a specific purpose, goal or end. Knowing the way in which computers work, how can they be used in library automation?—this is a true developmental question.

It must not be thought, however, that there is no likelihood that a computer system developed for a desired goal may end up unsuccessful. The state of our present knowledge of the fundamentals of the discipline precludes such certainty; we know too little about the computer, the environment and the infinite variations in situations—to say nothing of all the things we forgot to consider—to be entirely sure that a library automation system developed with such high hopes is actually going to work. This is part of the development process, with some success and some failure. After all, developmental work is an example of probability, not certainty. I am sure I need not elaborate here that the reporting of failures is a boon to others working in the field. With such knowledge they do not have to replicate errors in ignorance. Indeed, it reminds me of a cardiologist I know who likes to dictate his findings to his secretary while he examines his patient. "Negative findings are often good tidings," he says. "When I say 'heart negative,' I don't mean there's no heart in the body. Instead, I mean nothing bad has been found." Similarly, reporting errors and unsuccessful library automation programs may be the "heart negative" of our field.

Development, then, is the process of using fundamental knowledge to bring about some desired end. Within limits, based on reasonable hypotheses and sound experimental design, it is a trial and error process of fitting what is desired into what is known, of asking a few questions of the phenomenon, and then redeveloping the system to fit the new knowledge. It is a constantly iterating job in which one probes here, advances there, tries out one possible key to the riddle, retreats and tries another.

Uncertain development is the characteristic of newly developing fields, such as library automation, and the fact that some developments act as expected and others do not is a fact of life which must be accepted as part of the cost of doing business in it. It is not a disgrace; indeed, it may be the stepping-stone to a greater understanding of the fundamental nature of our intersecting fields: libraries and automation. What is especially needed, of course, in addition to a description of the projects which fail, is a discussion of why they failed, so that additional basic information on the nature of the problem can be obtained, and new iterations of the developmental systems can be undertaken.[7] Thus, out of apparent failure can come new success.

Conclusions

It is natural for people to wish to hide their mistakes, their poor judgments, their expensive slips. After all, it is the rare surgeon who publishes a paper, "Twenty-seven Appendectomies Performed by Me Which Ended in the Death of the Patients." Librarians share this emotion with everyone else, but they seem to be particularly prone not to report failures or endings of programs which started out with fanfare. Yet, thoughtful examination of such situations is an important step toward better programs in the future. It is therefore, in my opinion, the duty of those engaged in this field to document fully what they do and what they find they cannot do. Library automation is young, and as Thomas Henry Huxley put it, "There is the greatest practical benefit in making a few failures early in life."[8]

REFERENCES

1. Brodman, Estelle, and Bolef, Doris. "Printed Catalogs: Retrospects and Prospect," *Special Libraries* 59:783–88, Dec. 1968; and Bolef, Doris, et al. "Mechanization of Library Procedures in a Medium-sized Medical Library, VIII: Suspension of Computer Catalog," *Bulletin of the Medical Library Association* 57:264–66, July 1969.

2. Cayless, C.F. "Printed Catalogs or Catalog Information?" *Special Libraries* 60:413, July–Aug. 1969.

3. Brodman, Estelle. "Dr. Brodman Replies to Mr. Cayless," *Special Libraries* 60:413, July–Aug. 1969.

4. "One of the few libraries secure enough to admit that something it tried actually fell flat is the Hennepin County Library, which contributes to the exceedingly slim literature of project failure." *LJ/SLJ Hotline* 6:4, Dec. 19, 1977.

5. Salmon, Stephen R. "The Lessons of Problems and Failure." *In* Donald P. Hammer, ed. *The Information Age: Its Development, Its Impact.* Metuchen, N.J., Scarecrow Press, 1976, p. 210.

6. Bruer, J.M. "Acquisitions in 1972," *Library Resources & Technical Services* 18:174, Spring 1974.

7. Bolef, Doris. "Mechanization of Library Procedures in a Medium-sized Medical Library, XVI: Computer-assisted Cataloging, the First Decade," *Bulletin of the Medical Library Association* 63:272–82, July 1975.

8. Huxley, Thomas H. "On Medical Education." In *Science and Education.* Akron, Ohio, Werner, 1893, p. 306.

JOHN C. KOUNTZ
Associate Director of Library Automation
Chancellor's Office
California State Universities and Colleges
Long Beach

Problems of Government Bureaucracy When Contracting for Turnkey Computer Systems

THERE IS NO SINGLE or best approach to portray the idiosyncracies, real and imaginary, involved in contracting in most organizations. However, all this is simplified when the scope of discussion is narrowed to state bureaucracies, and becomes "duck soup" when the state is identified—which in this case is California. Furthermore, in the state of California if those goods and services relate to data processing, massive amounts of unnecessary research are replaced by massive amounts of wasted time interspersed with concentrated effort. This will not be a brief statement of experience, bracketed by remarks and followed by three questions from the floor and a smiling retreat. Instead, the following is a somewhat fictionalized account of real events, of things done by real people to each other. These people are still plying their trades, and many of these real events have yet to become history.

The state of California, although one devilishly nice place to live, is not quite as pleasant when it comes to doing business. Perhaps a brief walk through "the procedures" will clarify the situation. Then, to illustrate the full import of the procedures, we will follow an interactive process, just as in real life, to guide you toward a sensitive appreciation of your own purchasing department, administrative officer, etc. In fact, the guided tour will traverse "the procedures" five times, and I believe you will be better prepared to cope after this exposure. Also, in the interest of intellectual pursuit, you will gain an understanding of the hidden meaning of Sam W. Foss's fine poetic line relating to California, "Bring me men to match my mountains."[1]

The organization around which this pilgrimage perambulates is a department of the state of California. However, the sojourn touches as well on other organizational components within the state structure in a slightly convoluted manner, which resembles, most auspiciously, a wheel of fortune. Thus, it seems appropriate to represent it in graphic form as such a wheel (see Figure 1). Since interrelationship among the various participants is at a working level, the resultant structure evades simple Weberian explication. For the time being, it will suffice to say that the relationship is revolutionary, and, before embarking on this journey, to note that a vendor might come into contact with any of the various components.

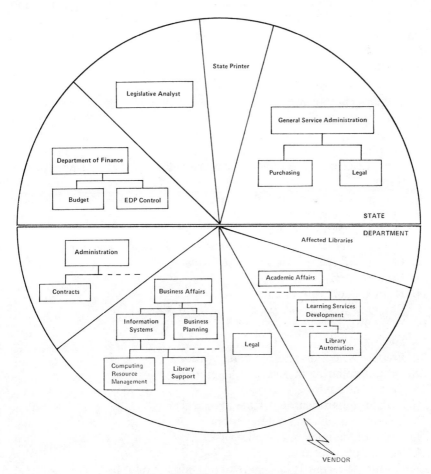

FIGURE 1. THE PROCUREMENT CIRCUS

Our objective is the procurement of what is called an off-the-shelf or turnkey circulation control system: a minicomputer with some mass storage, assorted terminals and the appropriate software to provide a computer-assisted property management system for our state/university libraries. The rules of the game are contained in: (1) the state administrative manual, (2) the current version of section 4 of California's annual budget act, (3) the state university's administrative manual, and (4) the Uniform Commercial Code. Further guidance can also be found in a volume written by Moses Maimonides entitled *Guide for the Perplexed,*[2] and a popular work sometimes referred to as the synoptic Gospels.

For a department of the state of California to buy anything even smelling like computers, the wheel is spun and all of the participants represented are brought into play. Such requests, rational or not, are immediately subjected to processing through the following twenty-eight steps:

1. Consult and plan
2. Obtain approval for the plan from the libraries
3. Prepare the budget
4. Sell the budget
5. Obtain department and state approvals
6. Obtain the budget
7. Prepare a purchase request or make it known that you need something
8. Obtain department and state approvals
9. Prepare a feasibility study
10. Obtain department and state approvals
11. Prepare invitation for bid document (IFB) and evaluation plan
12. Obtain department and state approvals
13. Release IFB
14. Hold bidders' conference
15. Respond to bidders' questions in writing
16. Wait for bids
17. Evaluate bids
18. Prepare selection and recommendation
19. Obtain department and state approvals
20. Sign contract
21. Obtain department and state approvals
22. Vendor installs computer system
23. Affected campus begins pilot use
24. Report on pilot use
25. Obtain department and state approvals for pilot use only
26. Obtain department and state approvals to begin procedure for next campus (if applicable)

27. Direct vendor to proceed to next scheduled campus (if applicable)
28. Repeat steps 22 through 28 (if applicable) for either the next "few" campuses or all campuses at the delectation of the control people (departmental *and* state)

The entire process can be interrupted at any point, and by almost *anyone*. One must then "take it from the top" or "downbeat." Interruptions may come from other vendors, in-laws, outlaws, casual spear carriers, parking lot attendants; all are empowered to grab the steering wheel—and have!

Although the steps outlined above are not entirely self-explanatory, they will be understood after having circled the wheel five times in an attempt to get an off-the-shelf/turnkey circulation control system. Bureaucracies are dynamic creatures and, since these five attempts span a 5-year period, one may expect assorted changes in rules and personnel; variety is, of course, the spice of life.

The First Attempt

In 1973, the planning and budgeting were completed, the words were written and the approvals obtained. Specifically, there were many meetings with library staff members, a workshop was held, and a "white paper" specifying the required functions was written by a committee of librarians. Concurrently, a feasibility study was made covering a pilot implementation and the subsequent installations of the system at all nineteen campuses; this was approved by the department's data processing procurement experts and their counterparts in the department of finance. An IFB was written and approved for the pilot and for subsequent installations, and an evaluation plan for bids was also written and approved. The IFB was distributed to approximately fifty potential vendors, a bidders' conference was held, and any questions which arose were answered in writing. Bids were received from nine vendors and were evaluated by a committee of librarians and members of the chancellor's office staff. From these a winner was selected and a recommendation report begun. Then a new man came on board as head of the department's data processing division.

The new man was not acquainted with the operations of libraries and, on meeting with the evaluation committee, found that the librarians were not data processors. As a result, he became anxious about a computer located somewhere on campus other than at the computer center. One objection was that such a computer would not be available for curricular support, thus depriving the students from data processing exercises. Almost instantly, the new man discovered his control agency role and communicated his reservations to all concerned. The resultant committee report aborting the procurement was, of course, approved. Time spent on this first attempt—from conception to abortion, so to speak—was nine months.

The Second Attempt

Following this first attempt failure were meetings, discussions, threats, promises, and a decision to make a second try. The previously prepared and approved feasibility study was apparently still valid (at least no one asked for a new one), but the IFB was completely redone for greater specificity. The project still required a pilot, with systems at eighteen campuses subsequently to be installed. The IFB was approved; an evaluation plan was written and approved. The IFB was distributed to approximately fifty potential vendors and a bidders' conference was held. Questions which arose during this conference were answered in writing. Right on cue, one of the potential vendors became cranky: "Why not use magnetic stripes?" "Haven't you heard of permanent magnetism?" "The sound emission requirement is the product of a. . . ."

However, cooler heads prevailed and Computer Universal Everywhere, Inc. reluctantly contemplated the faint possibility that we, the potential buyer, may have a vague idea about our users (a quarter-million budding Einsteins cheating the system through electromagnetic skulduggery) and about our working environment. ("You mean every time a book 'goes out,' that thing shoots holes in a piece of cardboard? Why, Doris will be driven mad!") The bids were received; Computer Universal Everywhere, Inc., having an extremely heavy commitment to magnetic stripes and loud equipment, did not bid. Several others did not bid either; in fact forty-eight of the fifty vendors elected not to bid.

In order to explain the next event, I must review briefly some of the mechanisms designed by the state of California to protect itself and its citizens from the nefarious activities of swindlers, blackguards and thieves. It is well known that swindlers, blackguards and thieves have pursued careers in either data processing or law, thus making it necessary to protect oneself and one's constituency from these shady rascals. In order to recognize early the imminent danger daily confronting the state's citizens, there evolved swift sure safeguards designed to cow all but those honest aspirants who would do business with the state.

These safeguards are hidden in the codes and manuals cited earlier and, for example, cause any procurement document which provokes from the private sector only a single bidder (i.e., fewer than two "qualified" vendors) to be suspect. This is what befell the second attempt. One of the two potential vendors asserted that (and I paraphrase): "Since telephone line charges may apply to the cost of the proposed system, and we are not the telephone company, we cannot freeze those line charges for seven years [the life of the contract], so the total cost of our proposed system may be subject to change." This flagrant lack of insight into the state's rules, regulations and procurement personnel (who believe that all honest firms do business on a fixed-price basis) was cause to disqualify the errant bidder. (I personally suspect that not even the offending firm was ever aware of its blunder.) Thus, there was only one bidder, and a procurement with only one bidder is unacceptable. Time spent on the second attempt: seven months.

The Third Attempt

After the accusations had subsided, and egos had healed, it was realized that the required system was still required. The war cry became: "Let's do it again!" Again, the same feasibility study was used, and more meetings with the librarians (to "firm up that specification") were held. Assorted communications with possible vendors took place (like trying to breathe novelty and excitement into a trip to the dentist), as well as high- and low-level meetings and strategy sessions in men's rooms—all the activities near and dear to the bureaucratic mind were undertaken, and were successfully completed.

The third IFB was released to vendors, a bidders' conference was held, and at about the time written responses to questions were to be mailed, a new lead programmer was hired in the Data Processing Division, but whose salary was funded by the Learning Services Development Division. This staff addition was deemed necessary because of the workload.

The new lead programmer also expressed almost immediate concern about this particular project. He reviewed the bid and evaluation documents and, finding nothing technical to attack, waited for the bids to arrive. Five of the vendors responded. A committee of librarians and the lead programmer evaluated the bids and selected a winner. Approvals were sought—almost.

The lead programmer had twinges of squeamishness. He felt that there was something (not technically) wrong about the winning vendor—something financially wrong. He discerned that the winning vendor would not last long enough to receive the contract in the mail, let alone deliver one system, much less nineteen. Essays relating to sound business practices were prepared, "acid test" ratios and schemes were developed to determine and predict the solvency of companies, and his past experience as an employee of a stock brokerage firm lent credibility to his concern. The firm selected was obviously a "loser," and was notified that it would have to exhibit unshakable financial backing in order to be permitted to do anything for the state of California. Meanwhile, a major automation dealer,

General Telephone and Electronics (GTE), announced its withdrawal from the computer market (following in the footsteps of Xerox, RCA, General Electric, Singer Business Machines and other fly-by-night companies). The lead programmer was promoted to supervisor.

I will not detail the bureaucratic process to which the selected "winner" was subjected. I will make only one observation: bureaucracies are paranoia-ridden, appearing to require red herrings as vitamins and scapegoats as entrées. The corporate "we" finally decided to scrap the procurement rather than go to the next lowest bidder (a possibility) because, after aggravating the original "winner," the corporate "we" feared that the "winner" would legally protest the selection of another "winner." Such action, while oblique to spectators, is known in bureaucratic terms as "asbestos trouser seats." Elapsed time was nine months. By now everyone involved had become financial experts, and the libraries got nothing.

The Fourth Attempt

In the summer of 1976 our Bicentennial was in full flurry, and somewhere in the state of California a small band of masochists were busily lighting fire crackers under their tails. By this time the IFBs for circulation control transactors had been cataloged in several libraries as an irregular serial, and librarians were wondering if the run was complete. To nobody's surprise, number four was released (and promptly received a call number).

In preparation for its release, high and low decisions were made; essays were written, refuted and refined; the virtues of high finance were acknowledged (a Chinese restaurant next door went out of business); and the drawbridge was lowered. There ensued consultations relating to what the libraries wanted; schemes to bar backyard mechanics, such as RCA, GTE, Xerox and others, from bidding; and the release of soothing memos between the department and state to assure all concerned that we were "on the right track" and that "any time now. . . ."

The pattern was retraced again: same feasibility study, same IFB, same vendor list, same festooning with approvals (with the new people at the state level asking: "What's circulation?"), a bidders' conference, written responses, bids, an evaluation, a winner, and then, for about five or six months, nothing. The winner had not really gone to sleep, it was simply reorganizing. A search party was formed to find the winner, since mere telephonic communications were inadequate, and they found the winner. What happened is not worth belaboring. As a result of the search party's ensuing encounter with the vendor, the contract was rescinded—mutually. Elapsed time from agreement to garbage heap: thirteen months.

Lessons learned: none. Gains attributable to the effort: the lead programmer was now an experienced supervisor building a staff.

The Fifth Attempt

By this time my unlisted telephone number had been leaked, and I was receiving threatening calls from irate, anonymous colleagues. I had the phone disconnected. The next few weeks were spent reselling the project to a variety of people. In cases in which the viewpoint was "I don't believe such a thing exists," field trips were made to libraries less sophisticated, but in more favorable procurement positions than our own. As a result, the popular refrain became: "Why don't we have something like that?"—and we were back on the track again.

Up to this point there was apparently an organizational feeling that the issue, like acne, was temporary; that the need for this system would somehow be outgrown. With the fourth failure, however, the state began to sit up and take notice. Like the Katzenjammer Kids, we within the department had been "doing it" to ourselves. Once a year we had had to sell the budget to the state, and year after year the state had bought the same program only to hear complex excuses at each year's end when the unused funds were returned.

Now, fired with enthusiasm, questions and vigor, we streamlined the specifications for the required system to attract more vendors. "What do you need a reserve book room capability for?" "Git rid ob dat noise spec!" "Cut those mandatory requirements." "Be less specific." Detailed meetings were held with librarians in which once-specific requirements became casual comments or were eliminated, and a workshop was held with the potential vendors to ensure that the new specifications could be met by all (essentially we returned to the specifications of the first attempt). Then we turned to the procurement itself to see if perhaps we had been asking for something in the wrong way. The conclusion was that we had, i.e., we had been asking for the time-phased implementation of all nineteen campuses, and this was inappropriate. Instead, we should be requesting implementation for a smaller number, with the option to add more later. (This would, of course, require additional feasibility studies and more approvals.) To the casual observer, these decisions may or may not make sense. To the individual with a vested interest in the outcome, to need something and to be eliminated by an arbitrary decision is significant. There were obviously complaints; remember, nineteen libraries were involved, and the pending procurement was arbitrarily limited to seven installations.

Business is business, and if a firm is to survive it must receive money for its products. A contract, purchase order or agreement for a multi-unit purchase, calling for delivery of one unit each year over a period of several years, and which is subject to cancellation at whim, *cannot* be sold to a bank—and banks, after all, have the money without which firms cease to exist. Limiting the number of installations, shortening the period of time over which those installations would take place, and providing for up-front cash payments following each installation neutralized most of the financial vemon encountered in the previous attempts. Cancellation by whim, however, remained a feature of the specifications.

It was a joy to write the amendment to the feasibility study. My attention did not wander during the bidders' conference, and when the award was made, it was to the same firm that earlier had been eliminated because it was expected to die momentarily. The process had reached step 23 and although we would see step 22 again (and again and again), we would not have to return to step 1, at least not until we had completed step 26.

Observations

I have singled out this struggle for a turnkey circulation control system solely because it is over. I could recount efforts to obtain on-line cataloging support, a union list of periodicals and serials, and other things (as it says in my job description) as required. These other examples, however, are either not turnkey, are still in process, or were done in-house. In all instances the same rules apply, and in most cases, circumstances arise in which the approvals required amount to several approvals from the same agency.

An example, without specifying a particular data processing item, may help. Let us say, for instance, that Good Guy Services is the vendor. Good Guy Services requires that funds be budgeted two fiscal years in advance. Assuming approval of the budget request by the department and the Department of Finance and Legislature for the fiscal year in which Good Guy Services is to be funded, a feasibility study will have been prepared and also assumed approved by the department and another office in the Department of Finance and Legislature. A purchase estimate is prepared. Since, in this example, Good Guy Services requires support hardware, two more estimates are required: one for the hardware and one for maintenance of the hardware. Bear in mind that although all these things will be provided by Good Guy Services, the services themselves are approved and controlled by one group of bureaucrats, the equipment needed to use the services is controlled by another group of bureaucrats, and the maintenance of the equipment is instantly delegated to anyone foolish enough to be at his desk at the time the "in" basket is emptied.

Each purchase estimate may require a separate bid cycle, or rationalization essay (if it is a sole-source situation), with subsequent approvals. Then a contract or contracts is required, bringing into play both the department's legal staff (to work out appropriate language) and the state's legal staff to review and approve. The contract(s) is then sent to the vendor to be signed and returned to the originating department. More "chop marks" are applied as the documents pass through final departmental review.

The entire process is then repeated at the state level, with different groups drawn into the picture (each group specializing in the individual products comprising the required service). Assuming that no one was on vacation, that all applicable documents were kept together during this convoluted circuit, and that the final "chop marks" were applied in synchronism, the services may begin. I can heartily assure you that in very few instances do things proceed in synchronism, or do all the documents remain together.

Drawn from these experiences are a few brief observations to provide guidance for what I perceive to be the situation in the majority of libraries. I believe they are self-explanatory.

1. Get your people educated in data processing (just reading a book about it does not qualify) through hands-on courses in which the permanent, professional staff members are exposed to the rigors of specifying and coding successful computer programs.
2. Do not attempt projects which take more than one calendar year to show significant, tangible results. Protracted projects have a high probability of turning sour and will either lose support of the librarians, the funding agency, or both.
3. Once you have set a project in motion, support it in a positive manner until it is completed. For those in multiple-institution organizations this may seem dictatorial. However, even though you may not have an immediate use for the targeted product, that does not mean others do not need it either.
4. Be able to specify in detail what you desire, and at the same time, be fully prepared to compromise those desires into a set of needs which the vendor can accommodate.
5. Remember that vendors require money to exist. Avoid parsimonious payment schemes and odd delivery schedules (e.g., contracts ordering thousands of widgets in quantities of one each at 6-month intervals will either provoke "no bid" responses or, if accepted by a vendor, will be treated with equal gamesmanship). The typical vendor, in the absence of cash, must have contracts (paper, in the jargon) which will support loans or can be sold (factored) to get cash.

6. Be aware of jurisdictional jealousies. Computers are magic devices. They may cause warts when not in computer centers. The data processors are understandably trying to save you from covering your body with warts. Knowing this, structure your viewpoint; by acknowledging the expertise and sensitivity of your technical colleagues, you may move together toward the desired compromise.
7. Have patience—or to paraphrase Sam W. Foss, "Give me patience to match these procedures."

REFERENCES

1. Foss, Sam W. "The Coming American." *In* Burton Stevenson. *The Home Book of Quotations*. New York, Dodd, Mead & Co., 1967, p. 56.

2. Maimonides, Moses. *Guide for the Perplexed*. M. Friedlander, trans. New York, Dover, 1904.

JAMES COREY

Systems Librarian
University of Illinois
Urbana-Champaign

The Ups, Downs and Demise of a Library Circulation System

THE AUTOMATED CIRCULATION SYSTEM discussed in this paper was in existence in the spring of 1978 when the fifteenth annual Clinic on Library Applications of Data Processing was held. The system was not a failure in the sense that it never succeeded in becoming an operational system. It did become operational and had functioned in the Undergraduate Library at the University of Illinois at Urbana-Champaign for two and one-half years (from May 1976 to December 1978). The system was stopped because it was replaced by a larger computer system that could perform known item searching by author, title and author/title, in addition to performing circulation functions. The university agreed to replace the Undergraduate Library system with the larger system as part of the negotiations for hiring a new director of the University Library.

Cessation of operation of the former system did not represent a failure of automation per se, i.e., manual techniques did not triumph over computer technology for circulation recordkeeping. Nevertheless, it still failed becuase it did not become a "convincing" automated system, one with a sufficiently strong reputation to survive in a time of rapidly developing automated systems for libraries. In addition to its one major failure—the failure to survive—the system encountered a number of lesser (but still significant) problems and failures during the course of its development. These are worth documenting in the hope that they will be instructive to librarians and library system developers who will be planning, building and installing systems in the future. The intent in documenting

35

this set of problems and failures is to seek out generalizations that could apply to other systems, indeed, to any system, whether a circulation system or other library system, whether commercially purchased or custom-developed. The details are important only insofar as they supply evidence of general classes of problems that could occur again. The selections that follow will describe the system in its operational form, summarize the history of its development (which is where the problems are to be uncovered), and conclude by extracting a list of generalizations that may be relevant to other systems.

THE UNDERGRADUATE CIRCULATION SYSTEM

This automated circulation system was functionally much like other on-line circulation systems. It could charge, discharge, renew, record holds for later borrowers, send overdue notices, compute fines automatically, bill for lost books, and record and report statistics. One advantage of this system over commercial turnkey systems was in the billing for fines and lost books. Fines and lost book charges were transferred in machine-readable form directly from the circulation system to the university's accounts receivable automated system, providing cost benefits both to the accounting office and to the library.

The host computer was an IBM 370/168. The library terminals were IBM 3277 cathode ray tubes (CRTs) which were used for all on-line transactions including charging, discharging and updating of library records. A leased telephone line carried the messages between the eight CRTs in the Undergraduate Library and the computer. Other offices and departments of the university also shared the same computer.

The system used three files: patron file, overdue file and book file. Patron records included their identification number (Social Security number), address and status (e.g., student, faculty, staff, or permit holder). Overdue records contained information about each overdue transaction (notices sent, patron response, fines, billing for lost books). A record for each cataloged item was in the book file. An arbitrary item number was assigned to each record, and each item was stamped with its number. Book records contained brief bibliographic and circulation information. Bibliographic data included were call number, author, short title, imprint date, status (such as "missing"), and the location of the book, such as "browsing area." Circulation information consisted of the item number, identification number of patron to whom the book was charged, due date, renewal information, reserve status, hold and restriction information, and counters to keep track of the number of times the book was charged or renewed. Records in all three files could be modified, created or deleted on-line from the IBM 3277s by staff with appropriate security codes.

As many as ten books could be charged to one patron in a single transaction. By typing the charge transaction code on the CRT, the screen displayed a fill-in-the-blanks charge format. On this display, library staff typed the patron's identification number and the number of each book being charged. This information, along with a computer-calculated due date, was immediately written into the book record file. As a double check, the computer responded with the call number and author next to each item that had been charged. Discharging was a similar process. When the discharge transaction code was entered, a formatted screen appeared on which up to ten books could be discharged at once using item numbers. Discharging removed the patron's identification number from the book record. Although bar coded labels and wands were not used, charging and discharging were nonetheless quite simple and fast processes.

When a book was overdue, the computer automatically created a record for the overdue file. Student notices for books four days overdue (the bulk of the workload) were computer-printed on continuous-form postcards. Successive notices were sent as form letters using information from a computer-generated overdue books report. Items which were eleven, twenty-five, and thirty-five days overdue appeared on this print-out. At the time of discharging, all overdue discharge dates were entered automatically in the overdue file, shutting off further notices.

Statistics on circulation were produced at regular intervals or on request, depending on the type of report. Charge statistics by patron type were produced daily and monthly. Special reports, such as the number of books charged each hour, charges by classification number, lists of missing items and items in special locations, were produced on demand. Statistics on books discharged by the hour were periodically requested to determine peak periods when more student assistants were needed for shelving. Tabulations of overdue books and fines by patron type were also generated routinely.

In comparing this automated system to the preceding manual system, the staff in the Undergrduate Library made several observations. They estimated that paperwork for circulation control was reduced approximately 75 percent. Overdue notices were sent much sooner, the first when the book was only four days overdue. With the manual procedure, the first notice had been sent when the book was two weeks overdue. Since patrons were reminded earlier, their fines were generally less. Billing of student fines became an automatic procedure, entirely eliminating typed vouchers. Patrons no longer had to fill out keysort cards to charge books, which reduced errors and speeded the charging process. Discharging was considerably faster on the computer because staff no longer had to search tub files for charge cards. The staff believed that patron satisfaction had definitely improved as a result of these new, faster and more accurate circulation procedures.

DEVELOPMENT OF THE SYSTEM

Preliminary Planning Stage: November 1965–December 1969

The preliminary planning stage of an automated system is generally characterized by discussion of alternatives, estimations of costs and benefits, visits to other libraries or conferences to discuss alternatives, and preparation of budgets to seek additional money to automate. Small amounts of money are spent on such things as staff travel to other libraries or conferences, but no new line item in the budget is established expressly for the automation project under consideration. The preliminary planning stage may be long or short, depending on the library and the functions being automated. For example, some libraries evaluated OCLC for years before they joined. Others took as little as six months from the time they first decided to consider OCLC until they had a budget and joined.

At the University of Illinois, the preliminary planning stage for the Undergraduate Library's circulation system took a little over four years. Preliminary planning began in November 1965, when the library's automation committee assigned the Automation Librarian to study circulation procedures in the Undergraduate Library. The Automation Librarian studied the library in spring 1966, but no recommendations were made at that time.

In June 1966, IBM entered the picture by assigning a company representative to study the Undergraduate Library's circulation procedures to determine whether it was feasible to automate circulation given the technology of the late 1960s. IBM's study was free to the library. (In the 1960s, almost all of IBM's data processing income came from the sale or lease of computer hardware. As a marketing strategy, IBM would frequently study a customer's operation free of charge, find automation "feasible," and generate income by selling or leasing hardware to the customer.) The study took nine months and culminated in March 1967 in a proposal to automate circulation with an IBM 1030 system connected on-line to an IBM 360/50 at the university's Office of Administrative Data Processing. Since the 1030 equipment read Hollerith punched data, students would need to carry Hollerith punched identification cards and the library would have to put book pockets and punched book cards in all circulating materials.

The library asked IBM for a comparison of off-line 1030 and off-line 357 systems with the on-line 1030 system. They responded with comparative cost figures for all three systems. Since computer usage costs were difficult to predict, estimates of these costs were supplied for the three alternatives. Computer charges for the on-line 1030 system were estimated to be nearly the same as for the two off-line systems, making the on-line system only a few dollars a month more expensive than the other two. Total recurring operational costs for the on-line 1030 system were estimated to be $3000 per month.

By November 1967 the library administration concluded that autmomated circulation based on any of the alternatives was more expensive than manual circulation. Furthermore, since a new Undergraduate Library building was scheduled for occupancy only nine months later in summer 1968, the administration agreed that automated circulation should be deferred until after the move to the new building. Accordingly, the library suggested a new date of summer 1969 for automating circulation. Circulation was expected to increase substantially in the new building, making automation more attractive by 1969, and the library accepted the on-line 1030 system as the best system to use.

Because the 1960s was a period of growth and prosperity for the University of Illinois (as well as higher education generally), the standard procedure for any new plan or program was to prepare a program justification report along with a request for additional funds. In March 1968, as part of the normal annual budget request cycle, the library requested start-up funds for fiscal 1969 and recurring funds beginning in fiscal 1970 to operate the on-line 1030 system. A few months later, the budget request was denied. For the first time in years, the refusal memo referred to "a period of declining budgetary funds which lies immediately ahead,"[1] and asked the library to categorize data processing requests as either "essential" or "helpful but not essential." Still uncertain about the cost benefits, the library classified the circulation system as helpful, not essential.

From mid-1968 until the end of 1969, the library went through a series of budget requests and reschedulings for the circulation system. System development was requested to begin in July 1969; then it was deferred to January 1970, then deferred again indefinitely. Budget requests were submitted to three different administrative levels, each requiring different deadlines for requests. The first requests were prepared and sent with the university's approval to the Illinois Board of Higher Education, the highest level and with the earliest deadline. On a shorter calendar cycle, budget proposals were sent to the university administration each year requesting money from the university's general reserve funds. Failing to get money at the two higher levels, the library asked the Office of Administrative Data Processing (ADP) to assign analysts and programmers from their existing staff to design and program the circulation system.

For eighteen months nothing succeeded. In February 1969, the middle of this 18-month period, the Automation Librarian noted that nowhere on the university campus was there an operational on-line system. Neither were there available personnel with the skills needed for implementing an on-line system. This lack of expertise may have accounted in part for ADP's unwillingness to assign personnel to the on-line circulation system or to support the library's budget requests. In April 1969 ADP demanded a comprehensive long-range library automation program before it would take a first step on circulation. The library said it could not prepare such a program without technical help from ADP. ADP said it did not have sufficient staff to do long-range theoretical studies. At this low point, the library's Automation Committee acknowledged an impasse with ADP and the Automation Librarian was granted a sabbatical to survey library automation elsewhere.

While the University of Illinois at Urbana-Champaign was getting no closer to an automated circulation system during 1968 and 1969, two university libraries nearby were developing the very system that the Undergraduate Library had been requesting, i.e., an on-line 1030 system connected to an IBM 360 computer. The Eastern Illinois University library, fifty miles south, developed its IBM 1030 circulation system in 1968, which became operational in September 1968, and has been running it since.[2] The Northwestern University (Illinois) library, 150 miles north, developed a generalized teleprocessing system in 1968 that could be used for all types of library functions. In 1969, Northwestern developed a circulation system using 1030s tied into the general teleprocessing system. Northwestern's circulation system became operational in late 1969, and is still in use.[3] Apparently, budgetary and technical problems were not insurmountable at these two nearby Illinois universities.

Development Stage, First Attempt: January 1970–June 1971

In December 1969 IBM renewed their marketing efforts. Seeing their proposals to sell 1030 hardware to the library rejected partly because of ADP's reluctance to assist with development, IBM offered, for a fee, to help the library develop the system. IBM offered its Systems Engineering Services (SES), their umbrella phrase for consulting, design or programming, at $28 per hour. IBM proposed three phases: (1) functional specifications, to be done entirely by IBM; (2) design specifications, done entirely by IBM; and (3) programming consultation with ADP which would do the bulk of the programming. The library, still indefatigable, submitted yet another budget request to the university to hire IBM as proposed. For the first time, ADP sent a supporting memo to the university administration, and in January 1970, the university approved the funds.

IBM worked on phase 1 from February to May, and produced a document of functional specifications for a charge of $3200. The functional specifications uncovered a need for terminal inquiry, so IBM 2260 CRTs were recommended as an addition to the equipment configuration.

In June IBM began phase 2, and the library requested recurring funds to begin operation of the system one year later, in July 1971. Staff at IBM, ADP and the library were optimistic that the system would be ready by mid-1971. In November 1970 conversion of the shelflist to machine-readable form began. ADP wrote a program to produce book cards and library staff started putting pockets and cards into the books. The university admissions office began punching student identification badges. Scheduled completion for the conversion was June 1971. Also in November, IBM completed phase 2, delivering a very thick notebook of design specifications. Hardware components specified were 1030s for charge, discharge and renew functions, and 2260 CRTs for the file inquiry and update functions. The specifications included record layouts, file structures, screen designs for the 2260s, message formats for all transactions, and flow-charts for fifty-seven programs. ADP spent two months studying the specifications and found a few inconsistencies and omissions which IBM agreed to correct immediately at no charge. By January 1971 ADP was ready to begin programming.

Then funding problems arose again. In January 1971 the Illinois Board of Higher Education cut the circulation system from the university budget for fiscal 1972. The campus said it could not, from its own general funds, support a full year of operations, but might support one-half year. Implementation was rescheduled from July 1971 to January 1972 to cut expenses. ADP decided to proceed with batch programming in spite of the delay and wrote twenty-eight programs between January and June 1971. Since there was no money for the on-line equipment (1030s and 2260s), on-line programs could not be tested, and so were not written. In June the project was suspended. The existing programs and documentation were carefully stored. The Automation Librarian, back from sabbatical, finished the university's required period of post-sabbatical employment and resigned.

Development Stage, Second Attempt: July 1971–June 1973

The library continued to submit the same budget request to the university, and through the university to the Illinois Board of Higher Education, from July 1971 to March 1972. As time passed, technological changes occurred. IBM introduced the System 7 minicomputer with 2795 data entry units for reading Hollerith punched data. The System 7 was intended to replace the 1030s, which IBM planned to withdraw gradually from their product line. IBM also announced the 3270 line of CRTs to replace 2260s. In March 1972 IBM's local sales office dusted off its proposal for the library's circulation system based on 1030s and 2260s and changed the configuration to a System 7 with 3270s. The cost for the new equipment was about the same, except that the System 7 had to be programmed. IBM assured everyone that the System 7 programming was minimal. Furthermore, the System 7, being a small computer, could serve the library as a backup when the IBM 360 was down. The 3270s were a newer, better line of CRTs and could be programmed as 2260s (emulation mode) or as 3270s (native mode). Since no CRT programming had been done, no additional CRT development costs were anticipated beyond the original estimates. The library immediately updated its budget request to the university using System 7 and 3270s as the new equipment for circulation.

The appearance of the new terms *System 7* and *3270* in the budget request must have had some effect on the university administration. Three months after the library submitted the updated request, the university provided partial funding for the project from its existing contingency reserves. The project moved again. IBM submitted two new SES proposals to do part of the on-line programming. One proposal was for programming the System 7; the other was for the IBM 360 on-line programs which communicated with the System 7. The on-line programming to communicate with 3270 terminals was not included in the funding, but was planned for a year later in July 1973. The library and ADP concurred and signed both programming contracts with IBM. IBM promised to be finished by January 1973 in time for spring semester.

The System 7 was planned for installation on ADP premises, four blocks from the library. Hollerith data collection terminals (2795s) at the library would be connected to the System 7 over a cable run through the campus steam tunnels. Investigation showed that the temperature in the steam tunnels exceeded the maximum recommended for the cable by 30°F. University electricians consulted with IBM, who decided that the extra heat would not interfere with data transmission if a different, better cable were used. The university ordered and laid the IBM-approved substitute cable in late 1972 at a total cost for cable and labor of $3900. Since this particular combination of cable and temperature had never been tested, the library worried about the decision, but acquiesced to the authority of electricians and IBM technicians.

In January 1973 IBM failed to deliver working on-line programs for either the System 7 or the IBM 360, but gave rosy progress reports saying completion was just a month away. In March IBM admitted the System 7 programs were not working, and promised to call in a company expert from outside the local area. Also in March, a new Automation Librarian was hired and began examining the system specifications. By May IBM had not found an outside expert, and local IBM personnel were still unable to make the System 7 work. Meanwhile the Automation Librarian had discovered a number of design flaws that affected both the on-line and batch programs.

IBM reassessed the situation, and in June proposed to complete the entire system for $85,000. According to this proposal, they would solve the System 7 problem, finish all of the on-line programs, and correct all of the design flaws in the twenty-eight batch programs which were already written. The library and ADP were incredulous. What was needed was IBM's completion of the on-line programs, as they had originally proposed to do six months earlier. The library and ADP jointly agreed to cancel the programming contract with IBM, seek a refund for money paid to IBM for programming (which was granted), and cancel the System 7 lease. The library and ADP also agreed to reevaluate the entire project, correct design flaws and resume work with just the library and ADP as project participants. However, as of June 1973, development had again come to a halt.

Development Stage, Third Attempt: July 1973–May 1976

Between July and September 1973, the library and ADP reviewed the design, modified record formats to correct flaws, and reviewed currently available circulation hardware. Since all books by then had Hollerith punched book cards and 35,000 students had Hollerith punched identification cards, the library and ADP agreed to try the System 7 again. The head of ADP wrote a memorandum to the head of the library promising a completed system in one year. Shortly thereafter, a new problem developed. A few months earlier the computer center had been divided into two separate organizations, with one group assigned to run the computer and its operating system software separate from ADP. ADP was left with the sole responsibility of applications programming. In October the two groups entered into a technical debate over which IBM teleprocessing software to use for the library's on-line system. One group wanted CICS, the other wanted TCAM. The debate lasted three months, during which time no programming was done. When the debate ended, CICS was selected. ADP had no training with CICS and, as a result, had to spend the early part of 1974 learning to use it.

From March 1974 to May 1975, the project was marked by slow but steady progress. All of the on-line transactions for the System 7 and 3270s were programmed. The batch programs were reprogrammed where required to correct design errors. The System 7 remained a nagging problem, however. It was not reading the data entry units (2795s) with consistency. Diagnostic tests were performed, and the results were not altogether surprising. The steam tunnel was, in fact, too hot for the cable, causing data to become garbled in transit. In August the System 7 was moved to the library to be near the 2795s. The System 7 was then connected to the IBM host computer over a telephone line, thus avoiding the steam tunnel. Since the cable problem had prevented a thorough test of the circulation functions, the library delayed changing over to automated circulation until the spring semester. The fall semester was planned for parallel run and test. Optimism was high that the last serious problem had been solved.

The optimism was premature, however. The System 7 was able to read the 2795s, but it began losing communication with its IBM host. The System 7 had been programmed to punch paper tape whenever the host went down—and it began punching paper tape with great frequency, even though the host computer was running fine. Within a week, the System 7 had punched several hundred feet of paper tape, enough to decorate the office area at the next staff party. Why did the System 7 think the host was down when it wasn't? ADP spent all fall trying to find out. IBM maintenance engineers checked and rechecked the hardware. In February 1976 IBM brought in a System 7 programming expert who located the problem: programming errors in the System 7 communications software supplied by IBM. IBM had recently improved the communications software, but the newer version was considerably larger. To use it, the library would have to lease a larger System 7 at a higher cost. At this point, the library made a bold decision to cancel the System 7 and rely totally on 3270s for all transactions. The 3270s had been working well for charges, discharges and renewals when the System 7 was down. Why not use 3270s all the time? The implications of the decision were considerable: 130,000 volumes had bookcards which would be useless, and the university would have wasted several thousand dollars punching student identification badges. With this key decision, the system jelled. In the two months remaining of the spring semester, the library disconnected and returned the System 7 to IBM, trained library staff on the 3270s, and performed a short parallel test. In May 1976, at the end of the spring term, the library cut over to the automated system. A few minor problems were encountered and corrected in the first two months of operation. Thereafter, the system functioned quite well.

COSTS

The two major cost components of the Undergraduate Library circulation system were development costs and recurring operational costs. Recurring costs ran approximately $40,000 per year, half for computer usage and half for lease of the IBM 3270s. By the time the system was shut down, rental credits had accrued on the 3270s to the point that they could have been purchased for about $20,000, leaving only the $20,000 annual computer use charge. Development costs relate to some of the problems encountered and are given in Table 1.

TABLE 1. DEVELOPMENT COSTS, 1970–76

IBM SES		$ 23,000
Hardware		
System 7		37,000*
Machine time on host 360		20,000
3270s		41,000
Student identification badges		19,000*
Shelflist conversion		10,000
University personnel		
Library		60,000
ADP		100,000
	TOTAL	$310,000

*Not used in operational system

The 3270 costs are the lease charges for the terminals during the developmental period before the system was operational. The figure for machine time is purely an estimate because costs for development time were not billed to the library and ADP did not keep the data; the figure of $20,000 is based on the guess that all of the machine time over a 6½-year developmental period equalled the cost of one year of operational machine time. Items marked with an asterisk were never used in the operational version of the system. Costs shown for student identification badges were the incremental costs for Hollerith punching. Since Hollerith punching was done solely for the library, these costs can be attributed directly to the circulation system. Half of the shelflist conversion costs went for punching book cards and placing them along with book pockets in 130,000 volumes. Since the book cards were never used, adding their half of the $10,000 conversion costs to the costs marked by an asterisk gives a total of $61,000 spent with no useful result. Costs for library and ADP personnel would have been lower if development had not been interrupted and delayed as it was, but it is difficult to estimate how much lower they would have been.

Under threat of a lawsuit, IBM reimbursed the university for the full $3900 in direct costs to install the System 7 cable. Thus, this cost is not listed in Table 1. However, the cable fiasco cost an untold amount in unproductive programmer time and months of project delay.

FAILURES AND GENERALITIES—BACK TO FUNDAMENTALS

The left column of Table 2 is a list of problems or failures encountered during the development of the Undergraduate Library circulation system. In the right column are corresponding generalizations that should be followed to avoid repeating these mistakes. Most of the generalizations seem so obvious that it should hardly be necessary to state them, but they are like fundamentals in athletics. Athletes are supposed to learn the basics of their sports at an early age and then progress to the more subtle fine points. Coaches find, however, that they must stress fundamentals again and again, even at the collegiate and professional levels of sports. The same is true with the generalizations in Table 2. They are fundamentals which, if not followed, will almost invariably lead to problems.

These generalizations are relevant for libraries purchasing turnkey systems as well as for libraries developing local systems. Librarians contemplating turnkey systems should not be lulled by turnkey

TABLE 2. UNDERGRADUATE LIBRARY FAILURES

Failure	*Fundamental Generalization*
No commitment	Obtain firm commitments from the administration before starting
Piecemeal budgets	Obtain the money needed to reach some level of operation
3-ring circus (library, IBM, ADP)	Reduce complexity; have clearly defined areas of responsibility
Took too long (hardware changes, data conversion inconsistencies)	Keep the project moving
Functions not fully understood	Obtain expert technical assistance
Too much hardware	Keep the system simple
Cable installation	Follow physical installation specifications
Did not survive	Build or buy "good" systems, i.e., ones that satisfy the need, impress the administration

sales representatives into thinking that problems can thus be automatically avoided.

The specific failures, listed in the left column do not "prove" in any logical sense the corresponding generalization on the right. One case does not establish a generalization, but there have been enough cases of the type listed on the left to establish credibility for the generalizations on the right. Even though very few problems and failures have been reported in the literature, many librarians have experienced similar situations or have heard about them from others. The problems encountered by the Undergraduate Library serve as documented evidence (probably very strong evidence) for the fundamental generalizations.

For the first year, the Undergraduate Library was committed to the circulation project, but the library administration was not. Then the library administration supported the project, but ADP did not. Without ADP's support, the vice chancellor remained unconvinced. It was not until IBM proposed in 1970 to do most of the work that ADP supported the project. With ADP's support of the library's budget request, the chancellor's office became convinced. However, the strongest commitment did not come until 1973 when ADP agreed to do the entire project without IBM assistance.

In the six and one-half years of development, from 1970 when the first money was granted until 1976 when the system became operational, the project received several partial budget allocations from the chancellor's office. Each allocation of funds had to be requested separately and the approval of any single request did not guarantee approval of the funds required to finish the project. Even when the system was nearing completion, the library did not know for several weeks whether permanent recurring funds for operational costs would be forthcoming. Projects do not move well under such tenuous budgetary circumstances. If a library cannot establish a solid budget with enough funds to reach an operational level, it is better to postpone the project until the necessary funds are obtainable. For example, at least one academic library purchased a turnkey circulation system, but lacked the money for a tape drive. The library thought the funds for a tape drive would come soon. The funds did not materialize. The library has been spending months keyboarding each patron one at a time into the patron file even though a complete student and faculty machine-readable file is available on the campus. Potential funding problems are not limited to locally developed systems.

At times during the first two development attempts in the life cycle of the Undergraduate Library system, the areas of responsibility of the library, IBM and ADP were not clearly defined. There were times when IBM and the library agreed to do something, only to have ADP learn about it later and point out a problem. IBM and ADP might settle a seemingly technical question, and the library would discover that the results were not what the library wanted. There were numerous phone calls from one party to another complaining about the third. The Undergraduate Library project did not make any steady progress until IBM had been removed and the number of parties was narrowed to two, with clearly defined responsibilities for each.

The Undergraduate Library circulation system took ten and one-half years to develop—four years of preliminary planning and six and one-half years of on-again, off-again development. The terminal hardware changed four times, from 1030s to 1030s and 2260s, to a System 7 with 2795s and 3270s, to 3270s alone. Considerable staff time that had been spent on planning, design or programming was lost each time the hardware changed. Conversion of the shelflist took three years for 130,000 volumes, because it too was started and stopped along with the rest of the project. Conversion staff, who were student employees, experienced very frequent turnover. With so many people working on conversion during the three years, interpretation of shelflist records was not consistent despite diligent training efforts.

The project was marred by two design problems. First, the functions were not totally understood by IBM when they wrote the design specifications. The IBM specifications were more than 95 percent satisfactory—close enough to pass the review of nontechnical librarians and nonlibrary computer personnel. If a trained automation librarian had examined the specifications in late 1970, changes could have been made before twenty-eight batch programs were written, and several thousand dollars could have been saved. (The fact that trained experts can also be important in evaluating specifications of turnkey systems has been acknowledged by one library administrator with considerable library automation experience.[4])

The second design problem in the Undergraduate Library system was in the hardware configuration. Too much hardware was specified. Originally the library was adamantly against keyboarding circulation transactions because they thought keyboarding would be too slow and error-prone. A 1030 system, a System 7 or a bar code system was regarded as a necessity. In the operational system, however, keyboarding did work and was not too slow. With the computer programmed to respond with patron name, and call number and author of each item, checkout was also not error-prone. The library staff found that the 3270s were simple to use and reliable. Hardware configurations can, of course, include wands for reading bar coded labels or guns for reading

OCR font and still work well; that point is not in dispute. But if the hardware is kept simple, the system will be easier to use and will malfunction less frequently.

One of the most obvious failures of the system was the cable. That $3900 cable is still in the steam tunnel, both shining ends dangling unconnected. IBM's payment of $3900 to the university did not recover any of the lost time and staff salaries. IBM's original recommendations for temperature range should have been followed and, although the company did approve the changes, use of the steam tunnel should have been avoided. However, physical installation specifications are complex and require a great deal of caution on the part of purchasers. The more one deviates from the physical requirements, the greater is the risk of problems or even of complete failure of a piece of equipment.

The most serious failure of the Undergraduate Library circulation system was the failure to survive. Although this system failed for political rather than technical reasons, if it had been completed sooner and extended to other branches, it might well have secured the support of campus officials.

The pace of change is now quite fast in library automation. In the future, increasing numbers of automated systems will be replaced by more sophisticated ones. If any automated system is to survive for a normal life span of five to seven years, it must be sufficiently functional and economical to win the respect of decision-makers in the library and in the university administration. Any system that fails to convince such administrators will risk the fate that befell the Undergraduate Library circulation system at the University of Illinois in 1978.

REFERENCES

1. Chaney, John F., Director of University Office of Administrative Data Processing. University of Illinois internal memorandum to Robert B. Downs, University Librarian, July 5, 1968.

2. Rao, Paladugu V., and Szerenyi, B. Joseph. "Booth Library On-Line Circulation System (BLOC)," *Journal of Library Automation* 4:86–102, June 1971.

3. Aagaard, James S. "An Interactive Computer-Based Circulation System: Design and Development," *Journal of Library Automation* 5:3–11, March 1972; and Veneziano, Velma. "An Interactive Computer-Based Circulation System for Northwestern University: The Library Puts It to Work," *Journal of Library Automation* 5:101–17, June 1972.

4. De Gennaro, Richard. "Doing Business with Vendors in the Computer-Based Library Systems Marketplace," *American Libraries* 9:212+, April 1978.

DOUGLAS F. KUNKEL
Computer Systems Manager
Washington Library Network
Olympia

So You Want to Build a Network

WARNING: BUILDING A NETWORK may be hazardous to your health. Depending on network philosophy and guidelines, networking may demand unparalleled cooperation and communication among libraries. If cooperation within a region is "unnatural," dissension and frustration are likely to discourage any efforts to develop a network promoting such ideas as resource-sharing and coordinated purchasing. Success depends on selecting objectives acceptable to the expected participants.

When designing a network it must be clearly understood from the beginning which capabilities will eventually be provided, so that the basic design is compatible with the long-term evolution of the system. Many problems stem from differing interpretations of network direction and philosophy. Network participants may be shocked or unhappy to discover either that their desires run counter to those of the network, or that the architecture of the computer system precludes certain capabilities. A common understanding from the very beginning will alleviate many subsequent confrontations.

This paper reviews some of the problems associated with selecting system characteristics, establishing a governance structure and managing the project, financing, and computer technology. Each section is headed by questions indicating the type of issues which must be solved. Examples are based on experiences with the Washington Library Network (WLN).

System Characteristics

What functional capabilities will be provided (single-function or multi-function)? Will the system be designed for a particular area of the library, such as technical services, or for a particular function, such as cataloging, or will several functions be integrated? If several functions are to be integrated, how many? Possibilities include acquisitions, accounting, cataloging, authority control, shelflist, reference, circulation, serials control, union catalog, interlibrary loan, and microform alternatives to the card catalog.

What types of libraries will be served (single-institution or multi-institution)? Will the system support the activities of one institution or several concurrently? If several, to what extent will one library be able to access information about another library's activities? Will the autonomy of any one library be usurped by the system under certain conditions? What types of libraries and related requirements will be accommodated?

What standards will be enforced (national standards)? Will the cataloging portion of the system utilize all of the appropriate indicators and subfield codes defined in the MARC format, or will a subset or other variation be employed? If MARC is adopted, how will compliance be enforced? The possibilities include "honor system," computer editing and human review. How will conflicts between local practice or choice of entry and the Library of Congress's (LC) practice be resolved?

What authority control will be needed? Will the choice and form of entry be subject to established authorities? If so, how will compliance be enforced? If several institutions participate in the network, will each have its own set of authority files? Will libraries be allowed to share a common set of authorities? Will sharing a common authority be required?

What aspects will be mandatory and what will be optional? What cooperative agreements beyond use of the computer system will be required?

The computer system will cost less to develop and operate if it is a single-function/single-institution system which does not utilize the MARC format and relies on the "honor system" for quality control. At the other extreme is the WLN computer system, which integrates all of the above-listed functions for an indeterminate number of institutions and is in strict compliance with the MARC format and LC practice (as required for all current cataloging performed by Washington libraries). Extensive programming edits bibliographic entries for proper use of the MARC format and routes them to a bibliographic center for on-line human review to ensure quality. Only one record is allowed in the data base for each unique item. Each authority group may have its own reviewers to ensure compliance with its established authorities. Multiple sets of authority files are allowed, with one or more institutions using a common set of authorities. Washington libraries have agreed to share one such set, making the union catalog consistent for the state.

Participants in WLN are expected to enter all new holdings into the data base. Therefore, use of the cataloging and authority control modules is required. All other subsystems or modules are optional; each library decides for itself the extent to which automation will be introduced. In addition, participants agree to share their resources with other members under reasonable conditions.

Unfortunately, when the previously developed systems and networks were surveyed in 1974, none were found to contain the desired combination of characteristics. At that time it was decided to develop a system based on many of the concepts embodied in the "quadraplanar" design planned for the University of Chicago's system. Financial implications of these design decisions will be discussed later; suffice it to say that selecting system characteristics has enormous impact on individual library procedures and organization, in addition to facilitating expanded programs in resource-sharing.

Governance and Project Management

Who governs the network?
Who signs the contracts and approves expenditures?
To what extent will participants be involved in decision-making?
Who sets development/enhancement priorities?
Who sets the prices for services offered?
What support staff will be required?

In 1973 independent requests to the legislature by three large state-supported institutions for monies to develop differing library computer systems provided the springboard for organizing WLN. While reviewing the requests, the Washington State Data Processing Authority concluded that one integrated system should be developed which would serve all libraries in the state. With the concurrence of the State Library, the first chartered organization, the Library Automation Committee (LAC), was established to serve as an advisory body to the data processing authority. Membership consisted predominantly of representatives from the three requesting institutions, with additional members from other types of libraries invited to ensure that the resultant system would meet the needs of all the state's libraries. LAC then decided what type of system to develop and established numerous subcommittees to collect and draft the detailed specifications for each subsystem. The committees functioned with little opposition until the likelihood of substantial funding added considerable credibility to the endeavor. At this time the jockeying for money and positions of influence began. LAC was attacked for not providing equal representation to all power groups, e.g., public, academic and community college libraries. Each constituency wanted its representatives seated on the committee. Some pressure was relieved by requiring equal representation on all subcommittees but in the end a few new seats had to be added.

Three years is not much time to develop a large on-line computer system and to spend over $2 million. Since the State Library had previously employed an outside contractor to develop a batch resource-directory system and had had excellent results, the decision was made to extend the contract and build upon that experience base. The advantage of that decision was immediate productivity on the part of the technical staff. The long-term disadvantage of the decision was that intimate knowledge of the system's internal aspects resided with the outside staff, not with WLN staff. Two full-time persons, a librarian and a computer system designer, were hired by WLN to coordinate system development and oversee the work of the contractors. Numerous staff members at the State Library combined with LAC subcommittee members to provide input on system requirements and to review system progress.

A major consequence of having only two full-time persons assigned to the project was inadequate communication between involved parties. Staff members were continually occupied and internal communications were thus too infrequent to keep everyone abreast of the current situation. Librarians throughout the state received insufficient information. It was not uncommon to be in a meeting where many attendees lacked the background to discuss the issues at hand. Frequent repetition of information known to some but not all was necessary to bring the group to a common terminology and understanding. An occasional group even operated on outdated information.

Midway through the development, about one and one-half years into the project, the state librarian retired. This event caused some loss of momentum while the new state librarian became familiar with previous directions, sifted through controversial statements on project status, and decided which past commitments were to continue to be honored. The arrival of a new top administrator also opened the possibility for reassignment of responsibilities. During the transition period, internal power struggles and uncertainty slowed decision-making and invited review of previous controversial issues. Previous decisions of the project leader were occasionally the subject of great dissension. Two-thirds of the way through development, the project leader left and the task of management fell increasingly on various committees. The main reason these turnovers failed to destroy the project was the relative stability of the staff employed by the outside contractors. Since the majority of the technical work such as programming was done by these outside groups, the project survived the periods of ambiguous responsibility.

Data processing groups unfamiliar with libraries frequently underestimate the size of the job by one order of magnitude or so. Also, on-line systems are more complex than batch systems. The estimating techniques which had worked well for projecting milestones during the previous batch resource-directory system proved inadequate for the on-line system, causing several major changes in the implementation schedule. Uncertainty as to when the system would really be ready caused some lack of confidence in the whole project, especially among those who, for whatever motives, privately hoped the network would never succeed. Due to schedule slippage and related cost overruns, the once-amicable relationshp with one contractor deteriorated into one of rigidity and legality. Toward the end it seemed the struggle had raged interminably. Despite the problems, however, the system was finally delivered, and contrary to predictions by the skeptics, it is working well.

In anticipation of the software delivery, the process of support staff recruitment began. Programmers with adequate backgrounds were located without great difficulty, but procedures estabished by the state's Department of Personnel caused more than six months' delay in the actual hiring of most employees. Recently, eight months elapsed before a planned promotion could be finalized. Inadequate staffing and the related lack of support in reducing hiring delays to less than one month remain very critical problems. That the system was developed and implemented by a small handful of people has to stand as one of today's modern miracles. It speaks well of the dedication of a lot of staff members and librarians throughout the state.

Complaints and general concern by librarians about LAC being attached to the Data Processing Authority caused the State Library to avoid bringing decision topics to LAC, and added incentive to efforts already underway to create WLN formally through special legislation as a permanent responsibility of the Washington Library Commission. Following extensive statewide hearings, legislation acceptable to the majority was drafted, presented to the legislature and passed. WLN as established by law is a self-sustaining agency of the state of Washington with the state librarian as executive director. Through this legislation the state is divided into service areas which elect representatives to a representative assembly. The assembly then elects an executive council, which in turn forms various committees to fulfill its advisory responsibilities to the commission. Governance of WLN is now participatory and democratic. Functions previously designated to LAC are divided between the executive council and its newly-formed committees. Membership in WLN is established through signing one of three types of contracts: (1) basic membership, in which the parties agree to participate in resource-sharing without using the computer system; (2) principal membership, stipulating agreement to share resources, use the computer system, and comply with established system guidelines; and (3) cooperative membership, in which the parties agree to resource-sharing while obtaining computer system services indirectly through a principal member.

Financing

How much will the system cost to develop?
What will transitional costs be?
Where will the money come from?
How many participants are needed to be self-sustaining?
How much can the network afford to lose during initial start-up?
Will development money have to be repaid?

Building a network of the scope and character of WLN is a costly endeavor. Raising over $3 million for system development over a 6-year period was a project requiring years of preparatory activity with the state legislature in order to create an awareness of library community needs. This was especially necessary since not all libraries participated actively in the process, and some even quietly worked for the demise of the whole effort. In spite of all the preparatory lobbying, funding was forthcoming only with the endorsement and active support of the Washington Data Processing Authority, an agency established to regulate the mushrooming expenditure of tax monies on computerization at a time when anticomputerization sentiment was strong in the legislature. This joint support, while successful in gaining the necessary development money, created an administrative awkwardness, i.e., joint responsibility for expenditures. In the early phases this awkwardness seemed a small price to pay for the apparent system of checks and balances which encouraged participation in the project. Occasionally, however, libraries got differing commitments from each agency which subsequently had to be reconciled. Fortunately, the money for development was allocated to a central fund, reducing the likelihood that a library would embark on a deviant course because of financial independence, and encouraging libraries to assemble and discuss ways to divide the wealth. Having the money in a common fund was a great stimulus to cooperation.

By far the greatest financial problem, second only to gaining the funding, was managing the budget. As mentioned before, data processors not familiar with library automation commonly underestimated both time and cost, and although the estimates in question here were made by personnel with considerable library system experience, the figures were repeatedly too low. Unfortunately, the overruns were rarely below $20,000, necessitating periodic high-level meetings to redo the budget. Throughout the whole project, energy had to be devoted to satisfying skeptics that there were no major scandals to be "exposed." In the end, more than $200,000 in unanticipated expenses had to be incorporated into the budget by delaying implementation and deferring certain capabilities, the later addition of which would not compromise the basic design.

Implementing the system required more money than development did. With continued support in the legislature it was hoped that money would be appropriated to cover: (1) the initial operating loss of the network, (2) the one-time start-up costs for participating libraries, and (3) the added transitional costs incurred by libraries switching over to the computer system. In an effort to encourage libraries to lower their operating budgets to pay for automation, the legislature granted appropriations only to the first two areas. This has created a dilemma for many state-supported libraries. Their options are (1) to spend the new equipment money in the hope that automation will pay for itself in cost savings, or (2) to return the equipment money to the state unspent and decline to participate in the network—at the risk of having to fund the full cost later. With one year remaining, there is still time for libraries to decide; however, at this time, the libraries are split on the question of participation without additional money for transition.

With over $3 million invested in development and implementation of the network, and a base monthly operating cost in the neighborhood of $75,000, one might question whether the return on that investment will ever be sufficient to justify the expenditure. While it might be convenient to justify the network as a research or pioneering effort paving the way for a new generation of automated library services, support for the system was gathered on the basis that participating libraries would be able to achieve a lower overall cost of operation. Several examples seem to indicate that the WLN system design will maximize the return on a library's investment in automation. For instance, the effort to establish and maintain a current publishers' name and address file to support ordering, claiming and paying functions in acquisitions will also support claiming in serials control and, if keyed by the publisher's prefix inherent in each ISBN, in reference assistance. The indexes for author, title and subject access to catalog information can also support the same types of access to on-order, holdings/location and circulation data. Through common access points, reference librarians can obtain information for all branches within a library and for all participating libraries in the region. Eliminating most manual files within a library will maximize the return on investment in computer filing. While a library may justify the use of the computer system for cataloging support alone, this system was developed to encourage much larger economic savings. Indeed, the investment is great because the system was designed to provide more economical library service throughout an entire region. The option is now available for libraries to make extensive use of automation in all areas of operation.

The degree of participation by each library will determine the total number of network participants needed by WLN to succeed financially. Fortunately, the legislature will not require repayment of the development monies, and having $1.2 million of initial capital has eliminated the need to recover all operating expenses when only a few libraries are participating. The challenge has been to establish a schedule of fees which will remain constant as the number of participants grows but will generate enough income for WLN to be self-sustaining when the initial capital runs out. Only time will tell if the WLN prices have been properly selected.

Computer Technology

What type and size of computers should be chosen?
Whose computers should be used?
What type of terminals should be used?
What design trade-offs can be made?
What data base protection is necessary?

Policy within the state of Washington requires all state agencies to obtain computer services from designated data processing service centers. The only decision WLN had to make was which service center to utilize. The initial decision was to continue with the same center used during previous development projects and which was also involved in ongoing operations. When that center became overcommitted and new equipment was not forthcoming, development was assigned to another computing center, while the first retained responsibility for ongoing operations. Finally, a comparison of rates charged by all service centers resulted in the decision to move all computing to a third service center located 300 miles away. The problems of development being done at three different centers, as well as the disruption of moving, obviously delayed implementation and added to the cost of the project. The establishment of a branch office for the computer system support staff 300 miles across the state has provided desirable isolation from frequent interruptions, but has also greatly hindered interstaff communications.

The state of Washington also negotiates master contracts for the purchase of computer equipment. Consequently, the first terminals used by WLN were custom terminals supplied by the designated contractor. The terminals worked well and were very satisfactory except for their inability to share a communication line to the computing center. Competitive price quotes for supplying custom terminals with the needed "multidrop" support resulted in a change of vendor which delayed implementation somewhat and required the changing of existing modems. Since the new terminals are programmable, considerable time was spent "debugging" the programs during their first year in the field.

Contrary to the situation ten years ago, existing computer technology was more than adequate to solve system design problems. The only real problems were errors of decision and constraints imposed by the use of commercially available software products, e.g., CICS and ADABAS. Errors of decision include installation of modems incompatible with the CRT terminals initially used by WLN, and failure to draft exhaustive specifications for custom CRT terminals. Software constraints imposed by CICS and ADABAS affected both system performance and functional capabilities implemented in the first version of the system. The performance-related problem, on-line response time, can be solved, given adequate time to work on it, but some of the unimplemented functional capabilities will require some ingenuity to reinstate. For instance, the bibliographic data base serves as: (1) a resource directory for all institutions participating in the network, (2) a union catalog for all libraries sharing the same set of authorities, and (3) an individual institution's catalog if its card catalog is closed. Searching the data base therefore requires an indication of scope.

There may be many items, perhaps millions, encompassed by any one such scope. Unfortunately, ADABAS cannot restrict a search to such a large set of records efficiently, so the scope option had to be temporarily removed pending development of an alternative.

As is the case with all new programming, numerous "bugs" were uncovered during the first year of operation. A few were costly to remedy (over $5000 in processing), but most were solved in a few days. The possibility of a catastrophic programming error always exists, although that likelihood diminishes the longer the system is in operation. To reduce the possibility that an error might be undetected, "snooper" programs were written to sample the data base randomly and periodically in order to verify accuracy of the relationships. In addition, duplicate copies of the data base are frequently made, and all updates to the files are logged to avoid being unable to recover from a major disaster.

Summary

Developing computer software for on-line library networks is very expensive, especially if the computer system is intended to support all functional units of each library and also to serve as a union catalog for the region. WLN has spent over $3 million developing its system. These monies were granted by the state legislature to develop a computer system which would curtail the growing costs of library operation. Recognizing that considerable research and "pioneering" were involved, and that an investment in new library technology was worthwhile, the legislature appropriated the money without any requirement for repayment.

Implementing the new computer system required formalization of a governance structure, and operating funds for the first two years until the system becomes self-sustaining. In both cases, the state legislature was again involved—first to create WLN through law, and second to appropriate $1.2 million of initial capital to be repaid later. Without the support of the legislature, it is doubtful that WLN could have found sufficient funding for such an ambitious undertaking. Ultimately, however, it was cooperation among libraries which convinced the legislature of the merits of a regional network and enabled development of a system to promote resource-sharing.

All the health hazards, disagreement, contention, anger, frustration, exhaustion, despair, and poor decisions which await courageous people who want to build a network are worth the risk if success will bring needed information to people and enhance the ability of libraries to make that information available.

R.J. BRAITHWAITE
Assistant Director for Network Services
Library Automation Systems
University of Toronto
Toronto, Ontario

Automation of the Catalog: The Transition from Cards to Computers

I WONDERED IF MY being asked to speak at this conference on "Problems and Failures in Library Automation" was perhaps a 2-sided compliment, as the University of Toronto Library Automation System (UTLAS) is one of the more successful projects in library automation in North America. However, in any automation project, no matter how successful, there are always some problems which can serve as lessons to others.

For instance, in the early days of the UTLAS project, we attempted to produce an on-line circulation system with complete stand-by facilities at every terminal. Each station was to have a badge reader, a punched-card reader, a keyboard printer and a paper tape reader/ punch. However, the project was abandoned after a pilot operating phase. Its requirements were far ahead of technology; it was a case of too much, too early.

Each component of this system was from a different manufacturer, and since this was before the advent of microtechnology, the entire assembly occupied a large desk. (Today most terminal requirements, along with a microcomputer, can be packaged in a desk calculator case.) The planned procedure was that the system would first read the patron badge and then the book card, and would produce a date due slip on the keyboard printer—much the same as today's systems. If the system went down, or the communications line failed—a not-infrequent occurrence—the paper tape punch would take over and record the transaction for feeding into the system later. Unfortunately, the effect on the library was at times devastating. The sound of the paper tape punch was more like a machine gun than a piece of library equipment, and it would start up without warning. Other problems related to the reliability of the central processor, disk storage, terminals and software. The decision was therefore made to abandon the project after the pilot phase rather than implement a system which had low reliability and a mean time between failures of about two hours.

With that out of the way, UTLAS pursued other developments which have been much more successful and serve as the foundation of current services. The UTLAS project began as part of the bibliographic system of the University of Toronto Library (UTL), and its other early endeavors included experiments with MARC and non-MARC holdings formats. Among these latter was the ONULP project, for which the University of Toronto Library prepared the initial collections for five new universities being established in Ontario. The cataloging data were converted to machine-readable form and a printed booklist was prepared. At least one of the five libraries is still using the data and format today; however, because the project had its own format which was not compatible with MARC, UTLAS did not develop it further.

Another non-MARC format was adopted for most of the holdings of UTL (about 1.25 million records). This presented some interesting problems when it became necessary to merge these records into a composite data base with records from several other sources, including some which were MARC-based. We kept in close touch with the Library of Congress (LC) system during the design of LC MARC and further developments were based on this format, including a service (which is now being terminated) for searching MARC tapes and producing unit cards or copies of records on magnetic tape.

At about this time UTLAS became a separate unit of the library and a new director with experience in the computer field was recruited. Work was begun on the development of an on-line system for inputting MARC-like records; this became known as LODES (Library On-Line Data Entry System). This system was further developed into LODES II where the entry process became an editing process, creating a system which could maintain a data base as well as enter in it. Further development of this system included revision of the format to bring it more in line with the LC and Canadian MARC formats, ultimately producing the system which is known today as CATSS (Catalogue Support System).

One of the biggest problems which affected UTL stemmed from these early pioneering efforts. The library held data in each of the formats of the early on-line systems, and used a non-MARC format for a batch system to collect a large portion of the data base. When the time came to make use of these data, the various formats had to be correlated with the current standards, and conversion programs were written to salvage as much data as possible from the earlier input. The cost of conversion has to be carefully weighed against the benefits. We have found that only with large collections of data is it economically justifiable to attempt automatic conversion from one format to another. In some cases, we have advised libraries to discard the results of a previous project and to start again. The second time around they are much wiser in setting up objectives and much more realistic about what can be achieved, so all is not lost. It is very unlikely that such an abandoned project will be written up as a paper, since it would require a very enlightened administrator to recognize the merits of "washing the dirty linen in public," even if the staff concerned were masochistic enough to want to invite public comment on their apparent incompetence or ineptitude.

With the UTL data base, it took an entire year for a team of two to three programmers, with considerable support from the systems librarian, to integrate the data from the formats into a data base from which a microform index could be generated to serve as an alternative to the card catalog. Even with all that energy expended, a considerable amount of work had to be done to clean up some of the data and coding problems that had occurred over the years; approximately 50,000 records have been edited to remove errors or to improve entries, principally with regard to filing rules. Some attempts were made to correct by program the lack of coding in the earlier data. For instance, honorifics were not coded fully; to correct this, the filing key generators were programmed to look for honorifics in the names and automatically generate the proper form. Unfortunately, computers are rather blind and obedient slaves. They were programmed to look for "Sir," "Lord," "Lady," etc., and they took the instructions literally; hence, John Sirica of Watergate fame became "Ica, John, Sir," and was condemned to obscurity as a misfiled entry. Tests are unlikely to point out such problems, for if a programmer foresaw their occurrence, he or she could have avoided them in the first place.

A related problem requiring careful attention is enforcement of the use of coding standards by the programming technicians, since the results of their efforts are not ᴐbvious until they become part of the final product. Then they may be only too obvious to the public, or more devastatingly, to the library procedures. One microcatalog had a large number of musical scores filed under "uartets" and "uintets" as the programmer was confused about which code indicated a traced entry. He wrongly chose the code which indicated the number of nonfiling characters. In a second case, a coder was mistaken about the use of hyphens and slashes in the holdings statements for serials. One indicated a continuous run of holdings in the serial while the other indicated a number of items bound together. When the data base was used to generate the item records for a circulation system, it was found that in some cases there was one record for a whole shelf of bound serials, while in other cases there were many records for only one item.

This instance raises another issue involved in planning for library automation. Many projects have been conceived to streamline a particular aspect of the manual system without first looking at the fundamentals of the problem. For instance, the card catalog should not be an end in itself. Its complicated structure was developed around the restrictions of a manual guide to a library collection. It was a vast improvement over the book or sheaf catalog; it is much easier to add cards to a drawer which is full by redistributing some to adjacent drawers than to soak pages overnight and repaste all the entries when a sheaf catalog page becomes congested. However, this does not mean that a card catalog is instantly up to date.

Data processing experts may encounter considerable problems with library data. They do not conform to nice, fixed record layouts but can vary in content and size as much as the books themselves. A title can vary from a single character to an entire essay. We had one "short title" for a pamphlet that filled twenty-two lines of a catalog card. This caused the formatting program to loop after completing the title just when it had to start a continuation card. It had formatted 22,000 cards before the operator killed the job because the computer was asking for the fifth output tape and only 4 tapes had been assigned to this type of run.

Another library had a contents note which exceeded 8000 characters and caused all sorts of problems. The largest record we have handled was over 44,000 bytes and prompted a reevaluation of all the size restrictions in our handling programs. They are now set to the system limit of 64,000. With this point in mind, careful consideration should be given to the claims made by some systems designers that allotments of twenty-five characters for author or thirty characters for title provide adequate clarification.

Another aspect of libraries that worries computer analysts is the size of the files. Many schemes have been tested on 1000 records or 10,000 records which would nevertheless collapse under 1 million records or more. Pauline Atherton's very interesting subject access project at Syracuse[1] generated index terms for 2000 monograph records and produced one of the largest inverted files that SDC had ever seen. This indicates that if we are to break out of the straitjacket of LC subject headings, system designers will have some complex problems to solve.

So far discussion has focused on the data base in the migration from cards to computers. This is the essential first step. The machine-readable data base is the basis of any alternative to the card catalog, whether it be printed, microform or on-line. Several users are currently looking at all three forms.

The printed book catalog has been used by several libraries as an alternative to cards, but as the booklists got larger, the printing and binding costs became excessive and this format had to be replaced. One of the most interesting of these book catalogs has been a project undertaken by a school library to use PRECIS indexing; this library is now experimenting with microform. A number of colleges, universities and public libraries are now regularly receiving microform catalogs. We have produced the first "infant" provincial union catalog for British Columbia. This is intended to become a complete union catalog of all holdings for the province within the next few years.

There is one other major problem associated with data bases concerning our authority facility, which will become operational this year: the availability of machine-readable source files. The subject authority file will be available soon (assuming LC resolves its problems with the issuance of the eighth edition), but there are no plans to provide a conversion of existing names in the foreseeable future. We see this as a major obstacle to the implementation of AACR II, which will have its greatest impact on the form of names. Therefore, we are proposing as an interim solution that some of our major user groups enter the cross-references from their card authority files; we would then link these automatically to the bibliographic records and generate skeletal heading records for all the names without cross-references. This plan is still in the discussion phase.

Another area fraught with problems might be termed "expectations of the users." This refers to the strongly held belief that the computer is a god and that its priests can do everything in no time at all. In reality, computer systems have considerable weaknesses that can be catastrophic if not compensated for in the system design. There are scores of examples of the fallibility of computer systems, such as astronomical electricity bills, and the unresponsiveness of charge account systems in correcting an error. These are the fault of the system designers who have overlooked the checking which in a manual operation would be done automatically by a clerk. However, it is often convenient to blame the computer. A blatant example of this was provided by a senior airlines official in defending the company's policies with regard to their charter class air fares. The system was set up so that there was a maximum of four charter class seats on any plane from Victoria to Vancouver; this was being challenged by a family of five who wished to travel charter class on the first leg of their planned holiday. The official stated that "the computer would not let them." However, not all problems can be blamed on the computer. One house-holder in England was so worried about his electricity bill that he turned off the power at the main switch, causing all the street lights on his road to go out.

Computer systems are not gods. They are very fallible and must be designed to survive all sorts of terrible events. They may not continue running when the lights go out, but they must not lose the data re-corded up to the time of the power failure. So it is a good idea to ask the system designer (if you have your own system) or the supplier (if you buy service or a turnkey system): What happens if I have a head crash or am unable to read part of the disk? May I continue or are the transactions after that lost? Do I have to return to the last security save?

Computer systems are expensive and time-consuming to develop. When preparing a manual system, all the unusual events can be omitted and the technicians can simply ask about exceptions later. In a computer program, however, every possible eventuality must be covered in advance or the whole process may fail and have to be repeated. Systems must be designed with the computer in mind rather than as an attempt to mechanize the manual process. The limitations of the card catalog may disappear, but new, computer-dependent limitations may replace them.

On the road from cards to computers, problems undoubtedly will be encountered, but many libraries have started and are making progress. Some libraries will go only part of the way to find that printed or microform catalogs will be adequate for their needs. How-ever, many will go all the way and provide a full on-line catalog, such as the University of California which is planning a 600-terminal in-quiry system to replace the card catalog.

Finally, I must congratulate the UTL staff in their forward ap-proach to automation. They may recognize many of the problems I relate here as theirs. This is not because they are worse than others, but because they have made more progress than others. If they had no problems, it would be because they weren't progressing.

REFERENCE

1. Atherton, Pauline. *Books are for Use: Final Report of the Subject Access Project to the Council on Library Resources* (Research Study No. 4). Syracuse, N.Y., School of Information Studies, Syracuse University, 1978.

J.L. DIVILBISS
Associate Professor
Graduate School of Library Science
University of Illinois
Urbana-Champaign

Problems of Teaching Library Automation

Introduction

I WILL NOT PRETEND that the sentiments expressed here are anything other than personal views arising from my teaching certain courses in the Graduate School of Library Science at the University of Illinois. It would be presumptuous to declaim on the problems of higher education in general, and boring to delineate problems specific to this particular school. Between those extremes, however, there are problems likely to be shared by other instructors at other schools, problems of some consequence to the library field in general. To deal with these problems candidly, I have not limited myself to "safe" topics such as the need for more money. If some of the "unsafe" topics give offense they should be understood in terms of bringing important issues to light.

Purposes of the Course

I might reasonably begin by considering what is to be accomplished in a course in library automation. In my own course I have characterized its purpose in terms of three major goals. The first of these is that the student become familiar with the uses of computers in libraries. This means not only exposure to existing and potential applications but also consideration of difficult and complex issues. Typical issues are autonomy versus cooperation, turnkey systems versus independent development, and the promulgation of standards. Students soon learn that many decisions in automation hinge not on technical issues but on ethical questions (the protection of privacy) or value judgments (the relative worth of two kinds of service).

The second goal of the course is that the student be able to read and understand a substantial body of automation literature. In more concrete terms, students should be able to understand nearly all automation articles appearing in general interest library journals, most of the articles in *Journal of Library Automation* and at least some of the articles from *Journal of the American Society for Information Science*.

The third goal of the course is that students be able to communicate technical requirements to programmers, systems analysts and other nonlibrarians.

The Problem of Understanding Technical Material

In order to understand the problems associated with familiarizing students with computer applications, we may profitably examine a representative application in some detail. The classroom treatment of circulation starts with general principles (control, information, statistics, associated services) and proceeds to the consideration of specific systems. One of the systems discussed is Ohio State University's Library Control System (LCS), a large, complex and sophisticated system that lends itself to classroom use. After a "guided tour" look at the most obvious system features we can look at the underlying structure of the system in order to understand its limitations and its possibilities for enhancement. Of course, discussion of structure requires familiarity with computer terminology (character, field, record, etc.) and computer equipment (terminals, disk files, etc.). Actually, establishing enough technical background to make discussion of the LCS system worthwhile requires the first half of the semester. But with that background it is possible for students to understand that the LCS master file consists of variable-length records hashed on call number into half track bins, and that there are multiple index files with pointers to the master file. (This concept takes perhaps an hour to develop in the classroom.)

Understandably, many students find this kind of material heavy going. The anonymous course evaluations at the end of the semester are often sprinkled with phrases such as "this is all so new," "too much background is needed" and similar indications that the course is too difficult. I have even been criticized because the "course required original reasoning." That peculiar complaint aside, it *is* legitimate to ask whether the problem lies with the material or with the preparation of the students.

Traditionally, library science has drawn most of its students from history, English and education undergraduate majors. We have seen a slightly broader range of undergraduate degrees in the past few years, but most of our students are still from the humanities and many find a technical course an abrupt change from the courses they have been taking. I am generally sympathetic to students who, for reasons of background, need to have the most elementary terms and concepts explained. At the same time, library science is a graduate program here and we expect graduate students to be resourceful and diligent.

People who go into librarianship seem generally to share a love of books and a service orientation. These are highly commendable qualities, but they are not sufficient for addressing the wide range of difficult decisions that face working librarians. Librarians at the management level must prepare budgets, allocate resources, evaluate systems and services of ever-increasing complexity, and make other technical decisions. A decade ago librarians had to be concerned with various methods for preparing catalog cards, but they did not have to consider purchasing a turnkey circulation system, or joining a network, or subscribing to an on-line information retrieval system, or installing an electronic theft-deterrent system. As technical issues of this kind continue to multiply, it seems certain that advancement in the profession will require a willingness to understand and work with the new technology.

An occasional problem is presented by the student with a lofty disdain for science or an undisguised antagonism toward all aspects of technology. It seems to be a peculiar characteristic of higher education that a person in the humanities can take perverse pride in remaining ignorant of the sciences, while a scientist would be deeply embarrassed to be ignorant of the arts. Perhaps this is a carry-over from the days when "real" education was education in the humanities, and practical skills were thought of in terms of the trades. At any rate, the student who feels that poetry is the essence of life and that technology is properly the work of uncreative drudges will find library automation unrewarding. It is difficult to assess the extent of this problem. Library automation is an elective here, so the student with an antipathy toward technology can simply ignore the course.

Students who have trouble with the materials sometimes ascribe the difficulty to its being "too mathematical." Actually, nothing beyond multiplication and division is needed, although even this may be too much for the student who had difficulty with high school math and has taken no math since.* The actual arithmetic is usually simple (and absurdly simple if a calculator is used), but its proper application requires a certain prob-

---

*The low point (I hope) was reached a few years ago when a student wrote on an examination paper: "I don't know how many zeros go after the 5 in 5 million. . . ."

lem-solving orientation. In other words, the problem is not in the ability to divide but in knowing whether the result represents books per hour or hours per book. The new math seems to have had negligible impact on this.

Problems with the Literature

The second major goal of the course, gaining familiarity with automation literature, suggests consideration of what kind of literature is useful in an automation course. To begin with, there are many fine introductory texts for computer science and business data processing. Excellent as these may be, they do not cover the problems of extended character sets, the archival properties of magnetic tape, the supervision of data entry, the negotiation of computer services, or a vast array of other topics important to librarians. In short, texts directed at computer science and commerce majors are of limited value in library school. Worse, I cannot point to an appropriate, high-quality text written specifically for the student of library science.

Several reasons can be advanced to explain the absence of good texts in this field. For one thing, the technology of library automation moves swiftly; a book dealing with hardware will be two or three years out of date at the time of publication due to the delays inherent in writing, editing and publishing. When the book is only a few years old, it begins to reflect the technology of an earlier time and has to be regarded as history. This point may be illustrated by consideration of how a book written today would differ from a book written five years ago in their respective treatments of keypunching.

There are other problems. Tact and the avoidance of lawsuits will generally compel the author of an automation text to omit some of the most instructive and entertaining material. As an example of this, in my course I describe an unsuccessful automation project at a large public library, all the while attempting to show the relative importance of technology, politics and personality in contributing to the failure. This particular project has been described in a generally worthwhile automation text but the book leaves a very different impression since delicacy and common sense dictated the deletion of any reference to problems. As a further example, I discuss the chaos that resulted at a large university when the administrative and research/instructional computer centers were combined into one physical facility with one staff. The problems there are not problems of hardware but rather problems of politics, personality, temperament and differing objectives. Issues of this kind are often central to the success or failure of a library automation project and they deserve extended discussion in the classroom. But the pressures that cause me to use the phrase ''a large university'' rather than naming the school (it is named in the classroom, however) also result in the most sensitive and delicate issues being avoided in print.

Of course, an author can always use a composite scenario or a completely fictional account to illustrate a point. Artificial examples may be better than nothing, but they tend to look artificial and they simply lack the impact of living, breathing, real-world case studies. In library automation case studies, by the way, truth really is stranger than fiction. I have seen and described in the classroom events and practices so bizarre that they could never be used in a fictionalized account.

Having noted the shortcomings of texts in library automation, we can now consider the use of journal articles in teaching automation. It is certainly easy to point to the shortcomings of journal literature—self-laudatory pieces, naïve reinvention of the wheel, opinion pieces masquerading as factual presentations, etc.—but journals still constitute a very important mechanism for keeping informed. The problem is thus not the quality of this literature, but rather teaching the student to recognize the wheat in the mountains of chaff published. My approach to this problem is to require the students to select a recent article and write a critique of it. Students generally read several articles in order to find one that they feel confident in reviewing and in this way they encounter articles that would never appear on a reading list. Many students are pleasantly surprised to find that they can read, understand and intelligently review a "technical" article that they would have skipped as "too technical" had they not taken the course. Moreover, most of the students come to realize that automation literature is quite extensive and ranges from the scholarly to the trivial.

Problems of Communication

The third major goal of the course is to enable students to communicate automation requirements to programmers, systems analysts and other nonlibrarians. This is a doubly troublesome area. The first part of the problem is that students often misunderstand the librarian's role in the design process. After all, can't the design simply be delegated to competent designers? The answer to that is a resounding *No!*—or at least it should be if the library is to stay out of trouble. Naturally, most of the students in an introductory automation course will never design a complex system, but they will need to select from competing systems; they will need to select features and options; they will need to describe design changes dictated by their circumstances; and they will need to write functional specifications. While doing all this, they should develop an understanding of what can reasonably be delegated. Librarians who delegate too much can be embarrassed by the result. Several years ago a large library created a book catalog and the only sorting rule they provided the programmers was that "&" should file as "and." As can be imagined, the resultant list was not in traditional library order and it required considerable effort on the part of the library to create a more complete and accurate set of rules.

In order to help students develop some skill in this area I require them to write functional specifications for some moderately complex product or service. Most recently, I have had them describe to a nonlibrarian programmer how they want a MARC record displayed on a CRT. (The premises are that the CRT terminal will replace the card catalog, and that the format must be suitable for patron use in a public library.) Reaction to this kind of assignment has been mixed. A representative from a turnkey vendor thought it was an excellent assignment and asked to see the better papers. The students generally regarded it as a terrible assignment. Excellent or terrible, it is a difficult task and for many of the students, a painful one. It has to be painful to spend hours preparing a multipage report only to have it criticized line by line. My hope is that they will be better prepared when the thing at stake is not a grade on a paper but a $100,000 turnkey system in the library.

The second part of the problem is that students vary in their ability to communicate clearly and effectively. They may have a clear idea of the feature or process they want, but experience great difficulty writing the requirement in terms understandable to a programmer or systems analyst. All of the usual problems of expository writing, such as misplaced modifiers and ambiguous antecedents, occur here, but two aspects peculiar to technical writing deserve special attention. The first is that students are inclined to use jargon unnecessarily. It seems unreasonable that a librarian asking a nonlibrarian programmer for a CRT screen layout would expect the programmer to understand the distinction between a secondary added entry and an alternative added entry, but students regularly make errors of this kind. It is all the more remarkable when one considers that most of the students were themselves ignorant of this distinction only a few weeks or months earlier. The closely related problem is that students seem always in danger of losing the "outsider" point of view. In order to see a new system or service in the way it will be seen by the naïve user or the occasional user, students may be required to remember how complex and confusing the library seemed before they became professionally involved. Or, it may be necessary to realize that intelligent, mature library users generally have very little understanding of how libraries operate (and, furthermore, there is no reason why they should).

Reluctance to Challenge

One of the purposes of an education for librarianship is to convey to the student a body of reasonably factual information, a purpose well understood by teacher and student alike. An equally important purpose is to impart a professional attitude, a way of dealing with the value judgments that underlie so many library decisions. There is, for example, no "correct" answer to the question: "Should I reduce the book budget in order to keep the library open later?" Questions of this sort are central to librarianship, but they cannot be treated directly in the classroom in the way that factual issues are presented. A primary difficulty in addressing this problem is that students tend to regard all the material presented in the classroom as factual and will accept without hesitation the most outrageous and idiosyncratic statement of personal opinion expressed by the instructor. To be fair to the student, the more technical the area the harder it is for the student to distinguish fact from opinion. I often find it necessary to append the caveat that I am expressing an opinion and that others in the field have differing opinions. It is not my intent to turn out a class of cynics, but students should recognize a value judgment when they see one and realize that someone else's value judgment is not necessarily more valid because it appears in print or is delivered from a lectern. In short, students are often reluctant to challenge the existing order (possibly because they fear it will make them less employable) and they must be given considerable encouragement to speak up.

Lack of Vision

Five years ago, when I described the OCLC network in class many students regarded it as an interesting development but not one likely to affect their careers. Today, of course, the significance of OCLC is obvious to everyone, but there are newer developments that may be viewed as likely trends or as science fiction depending on whether one is an instructor or a student. Again, to be fair to the students, they hear predictions ranging from the nearly obvious (networking will become more extensive) to the fanciful (the contents of the Library of Congress will be encoded on a thumbnail-sized chip). Without a strong scientific background it may be difficult to assess the plausibility of a particular prediction. The problem, however, is not that students have difficulty with technological assessment, but rather that they may reject out of hand any development that goes very far beyond their own experience. It is easy (and perhaps uncharitable) to ascribe this to lack of imagination, but I suspect that wishful thinking plays an equally important role. The student who is not comfortable with technology may consciously or unconsciously feel that the technological revolution will come to someone else's library. This is, of course, a highly unrealistic view, since technology is frequently thrust upon librarians for reasons beyond their control. In any case, the problem continues but it is not nearly as serious as it was a few years earlier. Possibly this improvement in attitude is a result of students seeing firsthand the sweeping changes that have been made and are being made in the University Library here. It is one thing to hear an automated circulation system described in the classroom, and quite another to sit at a terminal and browse the collection.

Solutions

The reader who expects all the problems cited in this paper to be resolved in the final paragraph will be disappointed. I will, however, mention two concrete steps taken by the Graduate School of Library Science to strengthen its degree programs. As the first step, we have actively encouraged undergraduates in the sciences to consider careers in librarianship. The number of science majors attracted through our recruitment efforts is modest but nonetheless adequate for the level of effort. It is not at all clear whether more aggressive recuitment would substantially increase the number of applications from science majors.

The second step has much broader implications. The Graduate School of Library Science has designed a 2-year MSLS program that will require students to take undergraduate-level courses in management, computer science and statistics (taken from other departments of the university) and will require library school courses in library automation and information retrieval. At this writing the program awaits approval by the university. It is expected that the inclusion of computer science and statistics requirements, together with the greater expense to the student of a 2-year program, will reduce applications. On the other hand, if the students who do apply for the 2-year program demonstrate greater dedication and better preparation, then strengthening the MSLS program will have been the right move.

KALPANA DASGUPTA

Senior Librarian
Indian Institute of Mass Communication
New Delhi

Problems of Library
Automation in India[1]

IN OLD CIVILIZATIONS LIKE India and other Asian countries, libraries have been in existence since early times. Recent political and economic developments which have brought about various types of changes in these countries are also reflected in the evolution of information systems.

India's educational system had a definite elitist slant in medieval times and the legacy of feudalism during the British period nurtured this trend. Libraries with very rich collections of manuscripts and other rare reading material were mainly the property of the elite. The infrastructure of the country was, moreover, not congenial for the kind of wide-ranged library system which one can envisage today. Library development has shown a marked change since 1947. It is estimated that India now has approximately 90,000 libraries of different types. The Indian library system can be divided into four broad categories: public, academic, special and national libraries.

Public libraries: India is divided into states, union territories, districts, subdistricts and villages. The state central libraries serve as public libraries. There are also district central libraries, but village libraries are few and far between. Libraries and library development are included in the broad category of education which, under India's constitution, is considered the responsibility of each state. Some states, namely Tamil Nadu, Karnataka, Andhra and Maharashtra, have very progressive library legislaton which provides the necessary framework and finances for developing good state public library systems. Despite this, only a very small percentage of the total population of India has access to public libraries.

Academic libraries: There has been some improvement in the standards and status of university and college libraries in recent years. At present there are more than 100 universities and 8000 colleges throughout the country. Most of these have library facilities which are in different stages of evolution. School libraries, however, have not been given sufficient attention. Primary and middle-level schools rarely have library facilities, and barely 20 percent of the secondary schools have adequate library facilities.

Special libraries: These are mainly the boon of the post-independence period. Government departments, research institutions, business and industrial houses have established libraries for their own research and development programs. Currently there are approximately 1500 of these special libraries in India; they are also at different stages of development.

National libraries: Under the national library system, the National Library of India is situated in Calcutta. There are regional libraries of national stature at Bombay and Madras. Some libraries on special subjects are now being given the status of national libraries, e.g., the National Medical Library and the Indian Agricultural Research Institute Library.

The major activites of the different categories of Indian libraries are mainly routine work, such as acquisition, circulation, management, processing, reference and bibliographic service, periodical holdings, information retrieval, inventory, and so on. The services and techniques utilized in the different libraries, however, tend to make these activities very cumbersome and slow. The acquisitions of most libraries are done independently, and involve unnecessary duplication of work and lengthy procedures. Cataloging and classification methods differ from one library to another and are generally time-consuming and labor-oriented. This is very confusing for the users as they must thus switch from one classification and cataloging system to another when using more than one library. There is also a lack of bibliographic control at the national level. The Indian National Bibliography suffers from a large time lag. Almost all library activities involve long hours of manual work, tending to make library service very unpopular. Therefore, users still cannot envisage a librarian as a giver of information but consider him or her a custodian of books. In order to improve the services of libraries, application of newer methods, such as information, computer and communication technologies, will be needed. I am only concerned here with computer applications in libraries and believe that for efficient functioning of our library systems, we will need automated services at some point. But serious thought must first be given to which areas will be automated, while keeping in mind the national need.

National Scene on Library Automation

Elaborate automated library systems are still far off in the context of any developing country. The priorities of each country may vary, but the emphasis is mainly on providing the basic necessities of life to its people.

The use of computers started in India with the establishment of computer centers at the Indian Institute of Technology and the Tata Institute of Fundamental Research during 1963–64. At present, there are about 400 computers installed at different places. The size and variety range from a Honeywell 400 to the large IBM 370/155 and DEC-1077. These computers are used mainly for scientific calculations, business applications and data processing for decision-making. Computerized library activities are found in very few organizations, and consist primarily of the use of spare capacity of available computer facilities suitable for off-line use.

Although the number of institutions which have computerized library applications is still very small, the awareness of quickly and easily available information is gradually increasing. I conducted a short survey in this connection through a questionnaire and personal letters sent to different institutions and business houses outside Delhi which have automated library facilities. Like most questionnaire surveys, this one did not prove very successful, although the personal letters I received from some heads of institutions were encouraging. I then visited some of these major institutions in and around Delhi, and interviewed many of those who work with computerized systems or have plans to do so in the future. The institutions visited were: Indian National Scientific Documentation Centre (INSDOC) and National Informatics Centre, New Delhi; Bhabha Atomic Research Centre (BARC) and Tata Institute of Fundamental Research (TIFR), both in Bombay; Documentation Research Training Centre (DRTC), Hindustan Machine Tools, Ltd. (HMT) and Central Machine Tools of India (CMTI), all in Bangalore; and Small Industries Extension Training (SIET) Institute and the Administrative Staff College of India in Hyderabad. Altogether, twenty-five organizations were contacted (see appendix). While this survey may not have been comprehensive in its coverage, the extensive discussions gave a good picture of the problems facing Indian organizations using library automation.

INSDOC, New Delhi: Automation is used for indexes (authors, corporate authors and subject), a union catalog of serial publications, data processing of Indian periodicals on science and technology, directory compilation, and the centralized acquisition of periodicals for thirty laboratories. The IBM 360 model 44 and IBM 1620 are used on a rental basis.

TIFR, Bombay: Automated operations include recent additions list, cumulative classified catalog of books, weekly list of preprints/reports of TIFR, catalogs of progress serials and periodical holdings, and evaluations of journals from the user's point of view. The CDC 3600/160-A and DEC-1077 computers are available in-house.

National Informatics Centre, New Delhi: Bibliographic citations are available so far only for books in its library; periodical articles are to be added. The center is a member of INSPEC tape service and a subscriber to a patent bibliographic information system since 1978. The HP 21/MX is used.

Indian Institute of Technology (IIT), Madras: In collaboration with INSDOC, IIT handled the CHEM/SDI project, a computer-based SDI system using the IBM 370 model 155 system and the CA Condensates data base. The CHEM/SDI uses a subset of CAN/SDI software made available by CISTI (Ottawa, Ontario) through Unesco for its regional pilot project. The project was also handled by NISSAT during 1976–77. The project has been upgraded into a national SDI service using CAC, INSPEC and Compendex data bases; there are more than 500 users.

DRTC, Bangalore: This group provides education and training, and researches methods for designing and developing computer-based information systems and services. A set of fourteen programs have been developed in COBOL for creation and updating of the data base, retrieval of bibliographical references in response to specific queries, provision of current awareness and SDI services, retrieval of factual data, provision of a referral service, the semiautomatic generation of a microthesaurus, indexing, and so on.

BARC, Bombay: The computer unit of the Library and Information Services of BARC uses the in-house computer Honeywell 400 and BESM 6 for information processing. Computerization activites include: preparation of a monthly current awareness bulletin, *Bibliography of Current Reports*; an SDI service offered regularly to some seventy-five users since May 1972; retrospective literature searches based on stored data on request from BARC scientists; subject bibliographies; documentation lists; compilation of periodical holdings; loan and issue system of the library; and inventory. An SDI service using the DEC-1077 computer of the National Centre for Software Development and Computing Techniques and TIFR and the magnetic tape output of the International Nuclear Information System is being developed and will be in operation shortly.

SIET, Hyderabad: This group has automated its Index to Product Profile, which is a list of literature available in the library to April 1976. A TDC 12 is used on a rental basis.

CMTI, Bangalore: Here work is being done on automating an in-depth index of periodical articles to compile a data base. They have a PDP/11 in-house. Future plans include classifying the trade catalog.

HMT, Bangalore: Currently under consideration is computerization of the comparative product profile and the issue system. The computer used is ICL 1903.

Physical Research Laboratory, Ahmedabad: This laboratory has a mechanized catalog of its publications holdings and information retrieval facilities. They have discontinued CAS and plan to start SDI. In use is the IBM 360 model 44.

Others: Some industrial units, such as Asian Paints India, Ltd., Hindustan Zinc, Ltd., and Institute of Armament Technology have automated catalogs of holdings.

Along with all these ventures in automated library services, a week-long on-line demonstration of the ESRIN/RECON data base system used at Frascati, Italy (near Rome), was arranged at TIFR during September 1976, with the assistance of Unesco and the European Space Agency. The Frascati center had 10 data bases and provided access to about 7.5 million references at the time.

NISSAT

Although these organizations and some other institutions have plans for future automation, the most important plan in India is the National Information System for Science and Technology (NISSAT). In 1971, for the first time, it was seriously felt that a strong national network of documentation and information services was necessary to meet the ever-growing need of scientists and research scholars. The Indian government created the high-powered National Committee on Science and Technology in October 1971. A report submitted by the committee in 1973 recommended the establishment of NISSAT under the Department of Science and Technology. The NISSAT network comprises a sectoral system, a regional system and other specialized services.

Sectoral system: All major areas of science and technology are classified into information sectors based on discipline, mission and product, e.g., leather technology, machine tools, drugs and pharmaceuticals, etc. Organizations of national stature, such as INSDOC, Defense Scientific Documentation Centre, BARC and Small Enterprises Documentation Centre, will continue to provide services at the national level.

Regional system: Because of India's size, more than one sectoral center for each discipline is necessary. Therefore, regional centers will act as NISSAT contact points. These will be located in major areas of research, development, educational and industrial activities, e.g., one center is in Delhi and another in Bangalore. Similar centers will be started in Bombay, Calcutta, Madras and Kanpur.

Other specialized services: Efforts such as the experimental computer-based SDI services of IIT and the on-line demonstration of ESRIN/

RECON at TIFR fall into this category. The ESRIN/RECON demonstration was a success and attracted considerable interest, and there is now a proposal to provide permanent terminals at Bombay and Delhi.

NISSAT also includes plans to create and maintain data bases on themes of national importance, and technical and statistical data banks on such topics as minerals, resources, etc. As mentioned earlier, NISSAT is the most ambitious information network plan in India today. Although the social sciences have also been brought within its fold, its emphasis is mainly on science and technology. Therefore, social scientists are of the opinion that a parallel system for the social sciences and humanities would make the circle effectively complete.

India's library system, as described earlier, can make use of automation in different ways for more effective functioning (see Table 1). Thus far, the specialized libraries and documentation centers have laid emphasis primarily on information retrieval, which has been substantially developed in many areas. The major need for computerized bibliographical control has not yet been satisfied.

TABLE 1. POSSIBLE COMPUTERIZED ACTIVITIES
FOR DIFFERENT TYPES OF LIBRARIES

Activity	Type of library			
	Public	Academic	Special*	National
Acquisition & distribution	X	X	X	X
Management & administration	X			X
Cataloging & bibliographies	X	X		X
Periodical holdings		X	X	X
Information retrieval		X	X	
Circulation	X	X	X	

*Special libraries include documentation centers.

Problems of Library Automation

Presently, the system of computerized library activities is growing, although it is still in its infancy compared with systems in developed countries. While at the sophisticated research level there appears to be general acceptance that computerized library activities will lead to increased efficiency, the hindrances to such a goal are many and any efforts to achieve it are the exception rather than the rule. Computerized library service is likely to be beset with technological, economic and attitudinal problems peculiar to most developing countries.

Technological Problems

Technological problems include both the hardware, i.e., the computer as an instrument for information processing, and the software, i.e., the methodology which is applied.

The major problems faced today in terms of the hardware are due to the variety of computers being used in different types of research and business institutions. The computers, manufactured by various firms (and even those of different generations of the same manufacturer), are not compatible. Developing countries sometimes receive sophisticated technology like computers as gifts from more developed countries; these often become obsolete from the manufacturer's point of view. Such machines are not only unsuitable for most complex work but any technical problems which come up cannot be repaired.

Information retrieval work requires machines more sophisticated than those manufactured indigenously, and few imported machines are capable of handling information retrieval applications. The random access facility and disks large enough for storage of bibliographic information are not readily available. In most institutions, organizational goals receive priority over the library's requirements, meaning that the librarian must use the computer available rather than what is actually required according to specifications. Library activities in all institutions are done through sharing disk space as well as computer time. Therefore, when the storage capacity is not large enough to accommodate various types of data, bibliographic data are given the lowest priority.

On-line facilities are rare in India. In fact, only TIFR's library has access to an on-line terminal for bibliographic data, the DEC-1077 computer of the National Centre for Software Development and Computing Techniques. The communication infrastructure of India is still not suitable for extensive on-line information facilities; the telephone system is not reliable enough to support an effective network facility.

Software problems arise because programs must be developed in terms of the machine on which they are to operate. Therefore, the incompatibility of equipment tends to make the software incompatible as well, especially when programs are written in machine or assembly language. While using languages which are not machine-bound, such as FORTRAN, COBOL, ALGOL, etc., may seem like a solution, in actual practice such languages cannot be interchanged without suitable modifi-cations. A software package developed for the IBM 360 model 30 would require many changes not only in the program but also in the program-ming language if it were to run on any other computer. Development of a program suitable for the available machine is therefore preferable to ac-ceptance of a package program. This makes the development and use of package programs difficult and leads to a lack of standardization in pro-gramming language as well as in output.

Machine-readable data bases are byproducts of international infor-mation network systems and are available on magnetic tapes. These are useful in building information resources and for retrospective search and current awareness services. Again, however, the tape service is expen-sive and suitably sophisticated computers are scarce. The data bases have a standard format which requires extensive changes to fit existing hard-ware and other system requirements. Also, relevant bibliographic infor-mation has to be selected from the data base and stored. Often this stor-age space is scarce and expensive.

Economic Problems

The major obstacle for any innovations in developing countries is the lack of resources. The initial cost of establishing a computer system is beyond the reach of most organizations and institutions. Library and information processing is done either with spare computer capacity made available by the institution itself (providing there is an in-house comput-er), or with computer time hired from another institution. The cost of hiring computer time and storage space is very high and often cannot be justified at the management level by cost-benefit analysis. At IIT, for example, CPU time per hour costs Rs.1000 for educational purposes and Rs.2000 for business and industrial use. Moreover, the computer provides only paper printout, and the paper often costs more than the processing (which runs approximately Rs.15/- per thousand lines). Few developing countries can afford the machine-readable data bases, either. The tapes are very expensive and because foreign exchange is involved in subscrib-ing to them, it is even more difficult for most organizations in India and other developing countries to afford them. The annual subscription rate of one data base is now $8000.

Library tasks often overlap and their peculiar nature seldom makes the advantages of computerization seem very convincing in the light of cost-benefit analysis. In India, libraries and information centers are at-tached to government organizations or research institutions, so library services cannot be calculated on a profit/loss basis. Long-term benefits have to be kept in mind while justifying such services.

The libraries that have computerized some of their services or operations often have not taken such steps as a result of serious thought. Computerization has a glamour of its own in the minds of many librarians. Overly enthusiastic librarians often run uneconomical programs, producing lengthy listings, for instance, in the name of computerized service. Often the manual method is used concurrently with the computerized system because of a lack of faith on the part of staff and users. The duplication of work and the cost involved in these cases is obviously unjustifiable; the librarian should know which aspects of service should be mechanized. An example of an economically viable computerized library activity is the centralized acquisition of periodicals in operation at INSDOC. This facility serves thirty laboratories, which not only frees the facilities from the tedious task of periodical acquisitions but also eliminates the cost of duplicate purchasing.

Attitudinal Problems

Computers appear very awesome to developing countries. They are powerful machines which can perform many functions and therefore offer a solution to the many types of manual inefficiency which often plague the developing countries.

Among librarians there are two different attitudes toward computerized facilities. One group is taken in by the glamour of modern technology and believes that computers can perform miracles. Members of this group often give insufficient thought to the real value of the computer to the organization/institution and make uneconomical, haphazard use of the facility. The other group, still the majority in developing countries, lacks knowledge of the potential and consequences of library automation. There is constant tension between this traditional librarian group and the "new-wave" librarians. Professionals of the majority group do not realize that computers cannot replace human intelligence. Due to the accuracy essential for data input in library services, the librarian/information scientist is indispensable. The National Library of Calcutta conducted an experiment to computerize the Indian National Bibliography in 1968. The scheme failed, however, because labor unions opposed it fearing retrenchment of library staff. Among developing countries, the attitudes of India's librarians are typical. They are not confident about automated services. Library staffs should therefore be trained in programming and thus be made aware of the work involved in automation. They will then realize that automation will not take away their jobs. They will also realize that computers are machines which have their limitations as well as their advantages.

The communication gap between the librarian and the computer specialist is another major hindrance in establishing any effective automated system in a library. There is often disagreement among the librarian, the programmer and the systems analyst. Librarians should be trained in computer programming and computer specialists should be versed in the special needs of library automation. Only then can a common language evolve among the three and a project be started.

Administrative personnel assume a very important role in decisionmaking. Their enthusiasm, support and conviction can help realize any new plan, just as their apathy and lack of understanding of the need for accurate and speedy information can jeopardize any effort. Although many things have taken a favorable turn in India, the majority of those at the management level unfortunately are not conversant with the development of information science and are unaware of the important role of information in all areas of national development. This very often results in insufficient planning, which in turn curbs the enthusiasm of imaginative information scientists and librarians. Due to this lack of appreciation, priorities are poorly ordered and funds are not well allocated. Administrators also have a tendency to underestimate or overestimate the capacity of automation.

Any information system or service is planned for the best possible benefit to its users. Unless the users are mentally prepared to accept a new system, however, it cannot be effective. Indian users are still unfamiliar and overawed by computers, so computer awareness and interest has to be fostered to enable proper utilizaton of a system. They should neither overestimate computer capabilities nor be afriad of interacting with the computer systems. Another obstacle is that, because batch processing systems are still in use in India, there are bulky printouts in monotonous type faces and formats which prove to be a headache not only for the librarian, but also for the user.

There is no dearth of manpower in systems analysis and computer programming in India. We are already exporting software packages to countries that find them less expensive than developing their own. Library automation is still neglected, however; it is an area which has not attracted young people with appropriate expertise.

Training should be given to both the librarian and the computer specialist about each other's functions and possibilities. Both INSDOC and DRTC conduct courses on automated systems in libraries. Under the forthcoming NISSAT plan, steps are being taken to build the requisite technical manpower. Moreover, the Indian government's Department of Electronics is developing training programs for the National Informatics Centre. There are two main objectives in training for library automation: (1) to orient the programmers and system analysts to writing programs suitable for automating library facilities, and (2) to persuade librarians to accept the utility of automation and teach them to prepare accurate inputs to make the system worthwhile.

Recommended Improvements

1. The computers used in India should not vary so widely. Production of computers with special capacity for library automation should be taken into consideration.
2. Government policy has taken a positive step in establishing large computer systems, with one sophisticated central computer capable of handling complex information to be connected to indigenous mini-computers. The National Informatics Centre project dealing with agricultural and other governmental data processing is designed along similar lines. Such plans should be pursued.
3. Indigenous, inexpensive library package programs are very necessary. These should be usable on a large variety of machines and be capable of handling different activities in the library. The MARC format would be ideal if it could be adapted for the smaller indigenous computers. DRTC is currently involved in preparing software packages for information retrieval.
4. The international data bases are being used by some organizations. However, these are expensive and often not applicable to Indian research needs. Indigenous data bases with our specific requirements should be prepared. Core periodicals in each subject relevant to India, and literature from important Indian periodicals, should be used as input for such data bases.
5. A national standard or common language for bibliographic information exchange is necessary. Efforts are being made to achieve a standard language compatible with any international standard.
6. Training of personnel, i.e., proper communication among the librarian, computer programmer and systems analyst is very important. Courses offering training in library automation are being taught, but there is a general need for better understanding among these three architects of library automation.
7. User awareness and orientation is very much needed. The users comprise managerial policy-makers as well as the research scholars and regular clientele of a library. The need for, as well as the possibilities of, automated library facilities have to be highlighted by professionals and experts in this area. A few seminars and workshops have been conducted at New Delhi and Bangalore, namely the UNISIST workshop in August 1975 and the Indo-U.S. seminar in 1977; however, little else has been accomplished in this area.

Conclusion

Do we need library automation now? In developing countries the problems are many and though they are not insurmountable, they are certainly very difficult to face and live with. The most pertinent question for our profession in this regard, however, is whether we really need computerized library services on a large scale.

A colleague from Bangladesh said: "The library and information sciences are a 'least-priority area' in this country. Only 20 percent of the people can write their names. There is an acute shortage of readers. . . . Most of the nation's resources are utilized for food, shelter, flood control and health problems." Although the Indian situation differs from that of Bangladesh in many ways, the first priority of any developing country is to provide the basic necessities to its people. Literacy and education are still at the primary level. Information of a very basic nature, such as the essentials for healthful living, must be presented in simple terms and communicated through media which will reach the people. Library activities of even the most primitive nature will not be within the intellectual grasp of most people unless the library is turned into a proper communication center. We cannot take as our model the community information center as developed in the West. The economic and social problems here are so acute and diverse that no one model for all parts of the country can be established.

As discussed earlier, library facilities may have to cater to a sophisticated and highly academic clientele in different organizations even though it is a minority. Libraries have had a long tradition here, but academia has yet to develop a tradition of data-oriented search for knowledge. The concept of libraries as storehouses of books remains very strong. Information is still sought in books rather than in microform. Because profundity in knowledge is the tradition of Eastern culture, the modern trend toward fast, accurate information is still not expected. That is exactly what a computer is supposed to provide for a scholar. Information is often treated as a commodity in the West. In industrially developed countries it is believed that any information which is economically profitable should be considered worthwhile and made quickly available. Can the same be said of the Indian situation? In highly developed industries, such as Hindustan Machine Tools, Ltd., a survey of the information needs of engineers revealed that the time factor was not important. Even if the information were received a day or two after it had been requested it would still be accepted and used. The competition in the industrial field is not sufficiently keen to require immediate information. Industrial research is done in a relatively leisurely fashion in India. At the documentation center of SIET, the need for computerizing library and information work has not been perceived. I quote: "As of today, there does not seem to be adequate justification for computerizing library and information work here. Our intake is not that sizable, nor are the demands on us yet so enormous that we should think of using computers."

The genuine need of the country is to provide usable resources for spreading literacy and to develop libraries at the school and college levels in order to give students the opportunity to acquire the taste for information. I do not intend to belittle the efforts to build a sophisticated information system such as NISSAT. India is a country in which the levels of development are varied in different areas. Its planners must therefore cater to the needs of each area in its own right. On the whole, however, our priorities still differ. Both librarians and clientele must be made information-conscious before anything as expensive, sophisticated and dumb as a computer can become a tool in their hands.

REFERENCE

1. I thankfully acknowledge the cooperation of all librarians who sent me very informative replies. I am grateful to Prof. Neelameghan, Mr. M.A. Gopinath and Mr. Devadassan of DRTC, Mr. T.S. Rajagopalan and A.S. Raizada of INSDOC, Dr. V.A. Kamath and Mr. N.M. Malwad of BARC, Dr. S.K. Havanur and Mr. M.G. Railkar of TIFR, the librarians of CMTI and HMT, Mr. S. Dutta and Mr. L.J. Haravu of SIET, and Mr. A.K. Dasgupta of the Administrative Staff College of India for their valuable interviews and suggestions which helped me in writing this paper. My special thanks go to Mr. Ali Sinai of Iranian Documentation Centre, Mr. Ashan A. Biswas of Bangladesh National Scientific & Technical Documentation Centre, Mr. Zultanawar of the National Scientific Documentation Centre (Djakarta) and Mrs. W.W. Sayangbati-Dengah of the Library of Political and Social History (Djakarta) for their kind response.

ADDITIONAL REFERENCES

Appukutan, N. "National Information System for Science and Technology (NISSAT)." In *Planning of National Information Network* (Papers from the Eleventh IASLIC Conference, Calcutta, 1977), pp. A45–A72.

Dasgupta, A.K. "Library and Information." *In* P. Gopalakrishnan and K.S. Narayanan, eds. *Computers in India: An Overview.* Bombay, Popular Prakashan, 1975, pp. 70–80.

Kumar, Girja. "Academic Information System in a Broad Perspective." In *Planning of National Information Network,* op. cit., pp. B63–B76.

Kalia, D. R. "New Challenges to Library Services in India," *ILA Bulletin* 11:16–20, Jan.–June 1975.

Malwad, N.M., and Kamath, V.A. "Problems of Computerized Information Processing in India," *Journal of Library and Information Science* 1:71–80, June 1976.

Neelameghan, A. "Information Technology: Applications in Development-Catalysing Activities in India," *Library Science With a Slant to Documentation* 13:75–84, Sept.–Dec. 1976.

Robredo, Jaime. "Problems Involved in Setting Up and Operating Information Networks in the Developing Countries," *Unesco Bulletin for Libraries* 30:251–54, Sept.–Oct. 1976.

Roy, A.K., et al. "Identification of Shortcomings in Existing Information Systems and Their Remedies: A Priority in Planning S&T Information Network in India." Paper presented at the Eleventh IASLIC Conference, 1977. (unpublished)

APPENDIX

1. Administrative Staff College of India, Hyderabad
2. Asian Paints India, Ltd., Bombay
3. Bhabha Atomic Research Centre, Bombay
4. Bharat Heavy Plate and Vessels, Visakhapatnam
5. Botanical Survey of India, Allahabad
6. Central Machine Tools of India, Bangalore
7. Centre for Development Studies Library, Trivandrum
8. Computer Society of India, Bombay
9. Documentation Research Training Centre, Bangalore
10. Gokhale Institute of Politics and Economics Library, Poona
11. Hindustan Machine Tools, Ltd., Bangalore
12. Hindustan Zinc, Ltd., Udaipur
13. Indian Institute of Technology, Madras
14. Indian National Scientific Documentation Centre, New Delhi
15. Institute of Armament Technology, Poona
16. International Institute of Population Studies, Bombay
17. Metallurgical and Engineering Consultants (India), Ltd., Ranchi
18. Mysore University Library, Mysore
19. National Informatics Centre, New Delhi
20. National Rayon Corporation, Ltd., Thana District, Maharashtra
21. National Sugar Institute, Kanpur
22. Osmania University Library, Hyderabad
23. Physical Research Laboratory, Ahmedabad
24. Tata Institute of Fundamental Research, Bombay
25. Small Industries Extension Training Institute, Hyderabad

H. WILLIAM AXFORD
University Librarian
University of Oregon
Eugene
and
LAVONNE BRADY AXFORD
Visiting Instructor of the Social Sciences Division
University of Oregon Library
Eugene

The Anatomy of Failure in Library Applications of Computer Technology

THIS PAPER IS AN analysis of a community college district's attempt to introduce computer technology into the operation of its five libraries. In spite of the fact that the conversion from the Dewey Decimal Classification system to the Library of Congress Classification (LCC) system, which initiated the effort, began about nine years ago, the basic causes of failure are as relevant today as they were then because they are rooted in the minds of those responsible for them: librarians, computer specialists and institutional executives. Involved in the project were five libraries serving the district's five campuses, a centralized acquisitions and processing unit (referred to here as library technical services or LTS) responsible for ordering and cataloging materials for the district's five libraries, and the district's computer center.

The efforts to convert to the LCC system, produce new catalogs for the district's five libraries, and automate the cataloging process were in every respect an unmitigated disaster for the 30,000 students in the district, the faculties of the colleges, and the taxpayers who unknowingly poured several hundred thousand tax dollars into the project and had nothing to show for it. The impact of the failure was particularly severe on the newest of the five campuses, which accepted its first class of students about a year after the Dewey-to-LCC conversion project began and entered its third year without a usable catalog to its collections and little hope of having even a minimally acceptable tool for at least another year. The only ones able to ride serenely through the lamentable episode were, of course, the administrators in the district headquarters who knew nothing about libraries as either technical or educational institutions, and who were unwilling to heed the advice of those who did, even after paying handsome consultant fees to obtain it.

This story is based entirely on documents produced by the individuals and groups involved in the conversion project. These documents include minutes of meetings of the planning group, project status reports, miscellaneous memoranda related to the project, and two consultants' reports, one commissioned before the conversion project got underway, and the other after its failure could no longer be ignored.

The story begins on February 19, 1969, when, after more than one and one-half years of argument and discussion, the instructional materials committee (IMC), composed of the heads of the four campus libraries,[1] the head of LTS and the vice-president for academic affairs, finally agreed to recommend the adoption of the LCC system to the president and governing board of the community college district. Since hundreds of libraries had previously followed this same path, the committee's recommendation was hardly noteworthy except for the unconscionably long time it took to produce it. Several factors, however, made it the equivalent of opening Pandora's box.

In the first place, the decision to adopt LCC was not really the result of a critical assessment of its merits as opposed to those of the Dewey Decimal system, but was rather an act of desperation, the roots of which lay in the failure of LTS to acquire and process library materials in a manner congruent with the needs of the four campus libraries—or of any library for that matter. The heads of the campus libraries and the academic vice-president believed that shifting from the Dewey Decimal system to LCC would somehow compensate for the lack of management and technical expertise which had crippled the operation of LTS since its inception.

The reasons for LTS's failure are all too common to the history of such organizations. The director had no authority to develop and enforce standardized systems, procedures and products. Everything the unit did had to be unanimously approved by IMC, which meant it had to cater to the idiosyncratic practices of all four of the libraries it served. In addition, the quality of the work produced was seriously deficient. For instance, when the librarian for the newest campus in the system arrived on the job, she found that books had been ordered for the "turnkey collection" solely on the basis of whether or not three of the four original libraries already held them, with no regard for changes in curriculum, or outdated or superseded material. She further discovered that all books ordered for the new library had their file access point determined by untrained student assistants, which resulted in multiple copies (e.g., one copy ordered under *editor,* two or three under *works,* and one under *publisher*) and that in creating the collection, no thought had been given to standing orders or to the need for back runs of journals and serials.

It is conceivable that inspired and competent management might have overcome to some extent the constitutional weakness of governance by a committee, but these qualities were sadly lacking at the time the conversion project was undertaken. In the face of these conditions, it is not surprising that at the time it was decided to adopt LCC, the un-processed backlog in LTS was approximately 11,000 volumes[2] and the average time between placement of an order by one of the campus li-braries with LTS and receipt of a fully cataloged and processed document was an unbelievable 502 days.[3]

Given this chaotic situation, and the magical qualities attributed to technology by the uninitiated, it is really not surprising that as IMC moved toward its final recommendation to adopt LCC, the computer loomed larger and larger in discussions of how to handle the conversion project and ongoing technical services operations. Thinking in this direc-tion had certainly been stimulated by the district president, who had communicated to IMC his interest in exploring the use of the computer to upgrade library services to students and faculty.[4] As IMC studied the problem of reclassifying 104,000 titles representing approximately 129,000 volumes, the computer began to emerge as the *deus ex machina* not only for creating the necessary new catalogs, but for overcoming the undeni-able performance deficiencies of LTS. The willingness to believe that it is possible to superimpose sophisticated computer technology over basi-cally inefficient manual operations and achieve anything other than chaos has probably caused more "computer failures" than any other variable; what emerged in the case under discussion is a perfect example.

Several weeks before IMC finally decided to undertake the reclassifi-cation project, the committee chairman had, in the course of a trip through California, spent "a few hours"[5] in the library of Foothills College, which had recently completed a reclassification project of 50,000 volumes. The project had taken just thirty-seven days and the computer had been used to produce book pockets and spine labels.[6] In a memorandum to the district president on his return (which in many respects is the key docu-ment in this case study), he noted that his visit to Foothills College "be-gan to open the door to a new look at the conversion project utilizing the computer."[7] It also opened the door to ultimate disaster. A project which for so many months had seemed complex and costly suddenly appeared simple and cheap. The typists in LTS would be trained as keypunch operators. The shelflist would be punched on tab cards. "Then," he continued euphorically, "the computer will enter the picture and provide us with conversion labels, catalog cards, book catalogs and any other service we may require. The actual conversion of our present holdings . . . will be done between semesters in the year 1969/70. . . . With the libraries closed (during the summer) and with adequate student help, we should complete the process in a crash program [before the start of fall semester]."[8] This reference to the use of student help is significant. After the conversion process actually got underway, both students and clerical help were employed to convert bibliographic records into machine-readable form without adequate training, supervision or checking operations. The result was that even had LTS and the computer center been able to solve the programming and hardware problems which plagued the conversion project, the quality of the resultant catalogs would have been so low as to make their production an exercise in futility insofar as the needs of librarians or library users were concerned.

Attached to the memorandum from the chairman of IMC to the district president recommending the conversion project was a tentative cost study of two alternate methods to produce the new catalogs for the campus libraries, one using xerography and the other the computer. For the former, the estimated cost was $92,000, for the latter, $24,000. Significantly, the figure for the computer-based alternative did not include the costs of software development, testing, debugging or computer time, and neither approach considered the costs to the campus libraries for such things as gluing on book pockets and spine labels and inserting book cards.[9]

Enthusiasm for the computer alternative permeated the entire memorandum. Not only would the computer produce byproducts not possible if xerography were used, but the unit cost would be approximately twenty cents per volume as compared to approximately seventy-one cents. The chairman of IMC had caught a glimpse of the best of all possible worlds. A computer-based project would not only be better in terms of overall benefits, but it would also be cheaper.

These cost estimates are a perfect example of the willingness of the naïve to believe in miracles. Less than a month before they were transmitted to the district president, IMC had rejected as unrealistic the per-volume conversion cost of fifty cents reported by Daniel Gore in the May 1968 issue of *College and University Business*.[10] However, once the computer moved to center stage, almost anything seemed possible—even a per-volume cost that was half what Gore reported. Later cost estimates eventually produced a budget for a computer-based conversion project of almost $65,000.[11] This figure, however, like the previous estimates, did not include either computer center or campus library costs, and it still projected a unit cost which IMC had previously rejected as unrealistic.

Lost in the IMC chairman's idyllic vision was any remembrance of the difficulties reported by the head of the Foothills College library with the computer aspect of its conversion project, which among other things forced the abandonment of the original plans for the book catalog. In a long description of the project sent to the chairman of IMC's Subcommittee on Planning and Development, edited here for clarity, the librarian wrote:

> Computer problems? They are impossible to enumerate. You name it and it happened. The programming was inadequate and the computer continually stuttered. The Dewey control number was used for producing the spine labels [book pockets and book cards]. At times, the computer would tear madly on for 100 labels printing an identical Dewey number with different LC numbers. If .5 was a good decimal, why not double it and make it .5.5? The big problem at Foothills was that the IBM people simply did not understand library terminology or needs, and they were more interested in what they thought they could do than in producing what the library said it needed.[12]

This last comment, born of firsthand experience, echoes a standard joke among computer users about IBM, which paraphrases John F. Kennedy's well-remembered plea in his inaugural address, "Ask not what IBM can do for you, but what you can do for IBM." Unfortunately, its implicit message to the neophytes in IMC about to undergo their first encounter with the magic machine went undetected.

Captured in the communication of the IMC chairman to the district president outlining the potential of the computer, and in the words of warning contained in the letter from the head of the library at Foothills College, are the primary causes of what is called, in a totally illogical way, "computer failures"; they are not computer failures at all, but the failure of human beings to use technology effectively. In spite of the fact that almost two decades have elapsed since the first large-scale attempt at Florida Atlantic University (FAU) to link computers and libraries, the attitudes which produce the human failures continue to exhibit a disturbing vitality. On one hand, there is the groundless enthusiasm exhibited by the IMC chairman with respect to the complexity and costs of computer-based library systems; and on the other hand, there is the equally naïve arrogance of the computer specialists who often promise more than they are ultimately willing to produce. To combine these attitudes with managerial and technical incompetence, which was the case in the example under discussion, will yield the inevitable result—unmitigated disaster.

About a year before the die was cast to opt for a computer-based conversion project and an ongoing automated processing system, IMC recommended that a team of consultants be hired. The recommendation was approved and a contract was signed with Donald W. Johnson, Assistant University Librarian, Arizona State University, and James M. Turner, Jr., Systems Analyst, Wisconsin State University at Whitewater. The consultants were charged with evaluation of "the [district's] processing center together with the possible applications of electronic data processing methods not only to the operations of the Center, but also to the member Libraries."[13] In May 1968, the consultants submitted their report. Had the district followed its major recommendations, it is possible that not only would a successful reclassification project have resulted, but a solid foundation might also have been laid for an eventual transition to some kind of computer-based processing system.

Although the consultants attempted in every way possible to cushion the impact of their findings, these were of such a nature as to make it impossible to do so. Their conclusions were as follows:

1. That the conversion could not be undertaken with any hope of success without a complete administrative reorganization of LTS.
2. That entirely new manual processing systems and procedures had to be developed with the necessary manuals in order to clear out existing and prevent future backlogs.
3. That a new head of LTS should be recruited nationally rather than from district personnel, and that this person be given authority congruent with the responsibilities of the position.
4. That only after all of this had been achieved should the conversion project be undertaken and planning begin for the eventual automation of the processing system.
5. That xerography should be used in the conversion project for the creation of the new catalogs for the campus libraries.

Insight into the depressing situation which the consultants found in LTS can be seen in one of their summary comments. "The picture we have painted," they wrote, "attended as it is with a host of recommendations, could incline the reader to the view that everything is now in such a mess as to be hopeless."[14] This turned out to be an extremely prophetic statement.

None of the consultants' major recommendations was acted upon. IMC, stung by having the deficiencies of LTS (and by implication, its own) clinically revealed, pulled into a defensive shell. Its appreciation of the report, forwarded to the district president on June 6, simply noted the desirability of beginning the reclassification project on September 15, 1968. Nothing was said about the method to be used.[15] Nine months elapsed between the submission of the consultants' report and the final decision to reclassify the collections and produce new card catalogs from an automated cataloging data base. It was during this period that the chairman of IMC visited Foothills College and came under the spell of the computer. The recommendations in the consultants' report (regarding the necessity of complete reorganization of LTS before considering the possibilities not only of automation but the reclassification project itself) were forgotten, and on March 5, 1969 the countdown toward disaster began. The budget for the project was set at $64,677 and the target date for completion—January 1, 1970.

The monthly status reports from the head of LTS to the district president and the governing board began on a predictably optimistic note and, just as predictably, progressively degenerated into a litany of mounting problems and extended deadlines, ending with the final collapse of the project two and one-half years after it was launched. At the end of the first month, the head of LTS happily noted that "no problems have arisen to alter plans for producing the card catalogs for the campus libraries between the first and second semesters of the academic year."[16] In the report covering the project through the month of August, note was made of the first problems with developing the necessary programming, and the district president and the governing board were prepared for the first extension of the January 1, 1970 deadline. The September report read:

> As we noted last time, our programming has been falling somewhat behind. Partly this has been because of the problems we have had in fully utilizing the "talent" at the Arizona State Prison . . . [nevertheless] at this point in the project, we still continue to move reasonably well and there seems to be no compelling reason why we cannot meet our calendar requirements of physically converting all present book holdings between semesters. The next three months will be critical, however, and there is always the possibility that we may have to change to the alternative plan of converting at the end of the second semester.[17]

The reference to utilizing the talent in the state prison refers to the fact that there were insufficient keypunchers in LTS and an effort was made to have some of the work done by the inmates enrolled in an ADP training program. The idea had merit, but only if the proper training, supervision and checking were supplied by LTS. These basic elements of an efficient processing system, as Johnson and Turner had pointed out, were, however, missing in LTS's own operations. Consequently, the prison keypunching operation only compounded the bibliographic chaos being created within LTS itself.

Within another month, the head of LTS expressed serious concern over not obtaining sufficient computer time to complete the project on schedule. After five months of the project, it was estimated that the printing time alone for spine labels, book cards and catalog cards would come to 318 hours, and that getting that much time on a multipurpose computer serving the needs of an educational establishment of over 30,000 students was going to be a major problem.[18]

The December status report confirmed the earlier hints of a rescheduling because of programming problems and the unavailability of computer time. The completion date for the project was reset at June 1970. Somehow, extending the deadline six months seemed to create the impression that the problems hounding the project would dissipate and the report ends on a new note of optimism: "As matters now stand," wrote the head of LTS, "everything is proceeding smoothly. . . . We should be ready on time."[19]

Three months passed and anxiety once again replaced optimism. The status report for March 1970 warned that "strenuous and extensive efforts" would be needed to meet the new deadline. This document is unusually significant in that it unconsciously reflects the growing sense of panic on the part of the head of LTS, the chairman of IMC, and the head of the computer center over the status of the project. In a budget summary at the end of the report, mention is made of planning for "disaster-averting contingencies" and the probable availability of funds to compensate for "legitimate disasters."[20] This latter phrase is intriguing. In mentioning the possibility of a "legitimate disaster," perhaps the authors viewed themselves cast in the role of the Greek tragic hero—good men doomed to destruction through no fault of their own. In any event, the concept presupposes that there are illegitimate disasters as well as legitimate ones produced by the attempt to unite computers and libraries, and that it is somehow possible to distinguish them. However, it is probably best to leave this kind of philosophical speculation to John Kountz, whose specialty is dealing with such semantic enigmas.

In June 1970 the project had entered its second year and the deadline for completion had to be extended again. This time it was set for the break between summer and fall semesters. The status report for the month also noted that the processing of current acquisitions (which had ceased a year before when the conversion project had begun) would soon be underway again and that the campus libraries could expect some completely processed material by the opening of school in September.[21] The librarians were to be as disappointed in their hopes of this as they ultimately were for the successful completion of the conversion project. As a matter of fact, the conversion project and its mounting problems absorbed most of the limited energies of LTS for the two and one-half years of the project's existence, and during this period, the flow of current acquisitions to the campus libraries was slowed to a trickle.

The months rolled by and in April 1971, two years after the conversion project began, the district president sent a memo to all concerned congratulating them on its successful completion. At an IMC meeting several days later, the representatives from the campus libraries demanded to know the reason for these congratulations, since they were still without usable catalogs and had no hope of receiving them in the near future. The head of LTS acknowledged that he had written to the president informing him that the project had indeed been completed, and he considered this to be so since the union shelflist was in the computer and three of the five libraries had recently received new individual shelflists. In his view, the catalogs for the campus collections were immaterial and besides, they would arrive in due time.

Obviously, the heads of the campus libraries could not accept this kind of self-serving sophistry and they expressed the view that it was incumbent on the head of LTS to clear up the misunderstanding which he had created in the president's office.[22] Since he was not inclined to do so, they were forced to take their complaint directly to the district president. They pointed out that not only were the campus libraries still without usable catalogs, but that even if all of the technical problems which plagued the project could be overcome, producing the catalogs from the unedited, error-laden data in the computer would be nothing short of a Pyrrhic victory. The district president was unmoved and supported the view of the head of LTS that the project had been completed; the fact that the campus libraries were still without catalogs was beside the point. (This incident in some ways is reminiscent of Art Buchwald's solution for ending the Vietnam War. All that was needed, he said, was for the United States to choose a propitious moment to declare itself the victor and then march off the field of battle.)

Nevertheless, it is probable that the complaints of the campus librarians had some impact, because shortly afterward, the district president invited Dr.Robert Hayes of the consulting firm Becker and Hayes, Inc. to audit the project. Dr. Hayes spent one day in LTS and submitted a report on June 4, 1971, stating that: "It is unlikely that the conversion project of your LTS division as presently scheduled will be completed as of the beginning of fall semester, 1971. The completion of the catalogs will probably require six months or more."[23] He proposed that the community college district engage his firm for a period of six months during which it would produce a "management program for delivery of catalogs, completion of backlog cataloging and management of LTS operations."[24]

Hayes's proposal is a particularly bothersome aspect of this case study. It is possible that his firm could have provided the management and technical expertise to produce the new catalogs within six months, but the question of whether or not it was worth doing was never addressed in his report to the district president. During his one-day site visit, the campus librarians had documented the unsatisfactory quality of the bibliographic data in the computer. Yet, in spite of this, he recommended producing the "base catalogs from the files as they now exist with corrections as they now are known."[25]

Several explanations are possible for this recommendation which ignores one of the fundamental weaknesses of the conversion project— the unreliable data going into the computer. The most plausible explanation, however, is the tendency of the computer specialist to believe that anything technically possible is always desirable. A similar situation occurred at FAU where numerous postmortem sessions with the director of the computer center failed to convince him that the technical accomplishment of producing the first computer-based university library catalogs was completely negated by the miserable quality of the bibliographic data they contained. The district did not accept Hayes's offer, and it is just possible that some perception of the soundness of the adage "garbage in—garbage out" had developed from the district president's confrontation with the campus librarians. Perhaps someone belatedly remembered the Foothills College library director's warning that computer experts are often more interested in what they can do than in producing what a library needs.

In any event, another year went by before the pretense that the conversion project and LTS itself were anything but a shambles was finally relinquished. By July 1972 the district had initiated a pilot project for purchasing book-processing kits from 3M Corporation and Richard Abel Company in an attempt to reduce the accumulated backlog of unprocessed material.[26] In addition, the largest library in the system was ordering its books directly from vendors instead of through LTS, and two other libraries were using the catalog of a nearby university library in order to correct the mistakes on the card sets supplied by LTS. In short, centralized acquisitions and processing for the five campus libraries had totally collapsed under the impact of the computer-based conversion project.

As a reward for presiding over the debacle, the head of LTS was given a sabbatical leave in the summer of 1972 to study for a doctorate in library science, and the head of the computer center was appointed interim head of LTS. His appointment was accompanied with both a mandate to investigate the causes of the inefficiency of LTS and the authority to take whatever steps were necessary to correct the situation. Since he was one of the important contributors to the disaster, the irony of his appointment was a fitting climax to the entire unfortunate affair. For three years students had suffered varying degrees of aggravation, frustration and deprivation trying to use libraries without adequate catalogs (or in the case of the newest library, without a catalog at all). For three years faculty had been annoyed, inconvenienced and distracted from their teaching. Much time had been wasted in fruitless meetings and probably more than one-half million dollars had been wasted in direct and indirect project costs.

The fundamental cause of the project's failure was incompetence combined with a bad case of narcissism on the part of the administrators, librarians and computer specialists involved. This was evidenced by IMC's rejection of the major recommendations of the original consultants' report which had forcefully pointed out the need to reorganize LTS completely under a new head, recruited from outside the district, before attempting the conversion project. An idea of the unfitness of this unit to acquire and process materials for five libraries may be demonstrated by the facts that, at the time of the consultants' visit, it did not possess a complete copy of the *National Union Catalog,* did not own the latest edition of the *Union List of Serials,* did not subscribe to *New Serial Titles,* did not maintain a subject authority file, and did not even have an automatic edge-gluer.

It is important to remember that the IMC chairman was the academic vice-president of the district who, on his own authority, could have recruited a new head of LTS with the kind of managerial and technical expertise which had been lacking since the day LTS was formed. Instead, he chose to believe that his perception of the situation in LTS and his own knowledge of the technical aspects of buying and processing books was more acute than that of the specialists he had called in as consultants. The same attitude came into play when he disregarded the advice of the head of the library at Foothills College to temper enthusiasm for a computer-based project with a critical assessment of what it would take to make it successful. It should be noted here that in spite of the problems encountered at Foothills College, a determined, hard-nosed, competent librarian succeeded in overcoming them, and that a major reason for her success was the absence of an overarching bureaucracy with the capability of stifling professional competence through its inevitable tendency to prevent anyone from "rocking the boat."

When the folly of attempting a computer-based conversion project without first bringing LTS to an acceptable state of efficiency became evident, it was impossible for anyone involved in the decision to admit it. Consequently, in spite of mounting costs and disastrous results, the project ground on until it died of its own inertia rather than through administrative action. As a sidelight, it is worth noting that in the summer of 1970, a library administrator and a computer specialist who had been closely involved with the failure of the larger and more complex computer-based library project at FAU joined the staff of a nearby university library. By this time, the conversion project was a little more than a year old and in serious trouble. Yet neither of these individuals was ever consulted about the causes of the failure at FAU or the lessons to be learned from it.

I wish we could say with some confidence that, as we approach the end of two decades since the first large-scale attempt to develop fully automated library systems, experiences such as the one just related are unlikely to recur. I cannot, however, as the attitudes which cause them are not easily eradicated. Of more importance is the possibility that failures in the future, the consequences of which will dwarf anything described here, may go unrecognized.

With the freezing of the card catalogs in the Library of Congress approximately two years hence, and with LC's implementation of AACR II, the era of the automated cataloging data base will finally have arrived. Many would argue that this landmark event in the history of librarianship occurred some five or six years ago when OCLC became operational, but the fact remains that for libraries subscribing to its services, OCLC is primarily a source of machine-produced catalog cards rather than a means of escaping both the escalating costs of maintaining card catalogs and the physical and intellectual limitations such catalogs impose on library users. In a sense, OCLC's brilliant success has had a mesmerizing effect on a large part of the profession by fixing librarians' gazes on the wonders of computer-produced and alphabetized catalog cards when they should be fixed on moving as rapidly as possible toward relegation of the card catalog to its honorable niche in library history. If we fail to move aggressively in this direction, it will be a computer failure born not so much of ignorance, naïveté and incompetence (as in the case study just presented) as of a kind of smug satisfaction and a desire to bask in the warmth of yesterday's accomplishments. However, despite its parentage, a failure of this nature will be no more legitimate than the one whose history has just been reviewed.

REFERENCES

1. The fifth campus did not open until Sept. 1970.

2. LTS. "Interim Progress Report," Nov. 2, 1968.

3. Results of a study of a sample of 100 orders placed with LTS in 1968, 1969 and 1970 by a district library, May 14, 1971.

4. IMC. "Minutes," Feb. 2, 1968.

5. Chairman of IMC to the librarian of Foothills College, Feb. 20, 1969.

6. Head of Foothills College library to the chairman of the Subcommittee on Planning and Development of IMC, Feb. 8, 1969.

7. Memorandum from the chairman of IMC to the district president, Feb. 2, 1969.

8. Ibid.

9. Ibid.

10. Gore, Daniel. "The 50 Cent Change—To Library of Congress," *College and University Business* 44:109–11, May 1968.

11. Head of the District Computer Center to the Academic Vice-President, May 13, 1970.

12. Head of the Foothills College library, op. cit., Feb. 8, 1969.

13. Johnson, Donald W., and Turner, James M., Jr. "Consultants' Report," May 1968, p. 4.

14. Ibid., pp. 23–24.

15. Summary of recommendations in response to the "Consultants' Report" forwarded to the district president by the chairman of IMC, June 6, 1968.

16. LTS. "Monthly Status Report," April 24, 1969.

17. IMC. "Monthly Status Report" to the district president and governing board, Sept. 18, 1969.

18. Ibid., Oct. 22, 1969.

19. Ibid., Dec. 11, 1969.

20. Ibid., March 10, 1970.

21. Ibid., June 18, 1970.

22. IMC. "Minutes," April 15, 1971.

23. Hayes, Robert M., to the district president, June 4, 1971.

24. Ibid.

25. Ibid.

26. LTS. "Monthly Status Report," Aug. 15, 1972.

CONTRIBUTORS

H. WILLIAM AXFORD is University Librarian at the University of Oregon. He has held similar posts at three other universities and taught library science at the University of Denver and the University of Illinois. In the past, Mr. Axford has served as President of the Library Automation, Research and Communication Association and has chaired several divisions of ALA and other library associations. He has published a book and twenty-five articles as well as served as editor for various library publications. LAVONNE BRADY AXFORD, visiting instructor of the Social Sciences Division at the University of Oregon Library, helped in the preparation of this paper for publication.

ROBIN J. BRAITHWAITE is Assistant Director of Library Automation Systems at the University of Toronto where he is responsible for network services. Mr. Braithwaite studied mechanical science at Cambridge and has recently worked with an international firm of consultants on a project involving the engineering, design and use of computers.

ESTELLE BRODMAN's interests in medical libraries and the history of medicine have led her to the study of scientific applications of information gathering methods, the impact of new technologies on these methods and the role the library plays as the communication center. Ms. Brodman has served as President of the Medical Library Association, Director of the Special Libraries Association and member of the President's National Advisory Commission on Libraries. Among her honors are the Gottlieb Award for Medical History and the Marcia C. Noyes Award for Distinguished Librarianship. She has taught at universities here and abroad and has published two books and numerous articles.

JAMES COREY is Systems Librarian at the University of Illinois, Urbana-Champaign. His experience in computer systems includes serving as data processing systems analyst for the University of California Library Systems Development program and as systems engineer for IBM. He has authored several publications on the subject.

KALPANA DASGUPTA, Senior Librarian at the Indian Institute of Mass Communication in New Delhi, has also served as librarian for the Indian Council of Agricultural Research, the National Council of Applied Economic Research and the Institute for Defence Studies and Analyses. Ms. Dasgupta was project director and editor of *Women on the Indian Scene: An Annotated Bibliography* and author of "How Learned Were the Moghuls? Reflections of Muslim Libraries in India," which appeared in the *Journal of Library History*. She has also coauthored a self-study guide on the urban problems of South Asia and a paper on mass communication presented at the Documentaton Research and Training Centre in Bangalore.

JAMES L. DIVILBISS is Associate Professor, Graduate School of Library Science, University of Illinois, Urbana-Champaign, since 1971. He is active in the fields of library automation and information retrieval and is a member of the Association for Computing Machinery.

JOHN C. KOUNTZ is Associate Director of Library Automation for the California State Universities and Colleges, and Chairman of the Technical Standards for Library Automation Committee of the ALA Information Science and Automation Division. As a member of ALA, he has been affiliated with library automation and electronic data processing for more than twenty-three years and during this period has established several small technical libraries and designed and implemented a total library automation system.

DOUGLAS F. KUNKEL has eight years of experience in the field of library automation. He is currently data base manager at Washington State University and previously served for four years as manager of computer services for the Washington Library Network where he was involved in designing the current Washington library system. Mr. Kunkel studied computer science at Washington State University where he implemented a student registration system and an on-line student record system. He is coauthor of a 1974 LARC publication, "LOLA II: An On-line Acquisition Subsystem (rev.)."

F. WILFRID LANCASTER is Professor of Library Science at the University of Illinois. His fields of special interest are information storage and retrieval, and the measurement and evaluation of library services. He has written several reports, articles and books in the field of library science; his latest publication is *Toward Paperless Information Systems*.

ALLEN B. VEANER is University Librarian at University of Southern California in Santa Barbara. He is currently a member of ALA, National Micrographics Association and Microfilm Association of Great Britain. His interests are reprography, micropublishing and library automation and he has published eighty-five articles, papers and books on these subjects. He has been editor-in-chief of the quarterly journal *Microform Review* since its inception in 1972 and was recently invited by the *London Times Higher Education Supplement* to prepare a critical survey of the application of microforms in American higher education.

ACRONYMS

AACR—Anglo-American Cataloging Rules
ADP—Administrative Data Processing
ALA—American Library Association
BALLOTS—Bibliographic Automation of Large Library Operations using a Time-sharing System
BARC—Bhabha Atomic Research Centre
CA—Chemical Abstracts
CATSS—Catalogue Support System
CICS—Customer Information Control System
CISTI—Canada Institute for Scientific and Technical Information
CMTI—Central Machine Tools of India
CPU—Central Processing Unit
CRT—Cathode Ray Tube
DRTC—Documentation Research Training Centre
ESRIN/RECON—European Space Research Institute/Remote Console System
FAU—Florida Atlantic University
GTE—General Telephone and Electronics
HMT—Hindustan Machine Tools, Ltd.
IBM—International Business Machines
IFB—Invitation for Bid
IIT—Indian Institute of Technology
IMC—Instructional Materials Committee
INSDOC—Indian National Scientifc Documentation Centre
INSPEC—Information Service for Physics Electrotechnology and Control
ISBN—International Standard Book Number
LAC—Library Automation Committee
LC—Library of Congress
LCC—Library of Congress Classification
LCS—Library Control System
LODES—Library On-line Data Entry System
LTS—Library Technical Services
MARC—Machine-Readable Cataloging
MSLS—Master of Science in Library Science
NASA—National Aeronautics and Space Administration
NISSAT—National Information System for Science and Technology
OCLC—Ohio College Library Center
OCR—Optical Character Reader
ONULP—Ontario New Universities Library Project

PRECIS—Preserved Context Index System
RCA—Radio Corporation of America
SDC—Systems Development Corporation
SDI—Selective Dissemination of Information
SES—Systems Engineering Services
SIET—Small Industries Extension Training
TCAM—Telecommunications Access Method
TIFR—Tata Institute of Fundamental Research
UNISIST—World Science Information System
UTL—University of Toronto Library
UTLAS—University of Toronto Library Automation System
WLN—Washington Library Network

INDEX

AACR II, 64, 101.

Academic libraries in India, 76.

ADABAS (software package), 58.

Authority control, 9, 52, 64.

Automated libraries in India, 77–79.

Automated systems: comparison with manual systems, 37, 39, 65.

Automation: zeal of newly converted, 17–19; in India, attitudinal problems with, 83–85.

BALLOTS, 7.

Bibliographic control: and real needs of library patrons, 9; role of computers in, 10; ideal of International Institute of Bibliography, 12.

Bibliographic data: problems in automation, 62–63. See also Conversion of catalog records to machine-readable form.

Bibliographic systems: isolation from society, 13, 14.

Bidding: as a part of procurement process, 26–30 passim, 32.

Budgets, 39, 41, 47, 56.

Bureaucracies, state: and contracts, 24–34 passim.

Cable, telecommunication. See Telecommunication cable.

California: contracting for automated circulation in, 24–34.

Cataloging system, computer based: report of failure, 16. See also Failures in library automation.

Catalogs: labor costs of, 10; closure of, 10; and perfectionism, 10; cosmetic aspects of, 10–11.

CATSS, 61.

CICS (software package), 43, 58.

Circulation systems: purchase of turnkey, 24–34; development at U. of Illinois, 35–49; use of IBM equipment in, 36; files used in, 36; overdue procedures of, 37; statistics for, 37; problems with turnkey, 46–47; flaws in design of, 48; at U. of Toronto, 60–61; in course on library automation, 68.

Communication formats: problems with, 61–62; conversion of, 62. See also MARC.

Communication gap between librarians and technicians, 71–72, 83–84.

Computer terminals: custom made, in WLN, 58. See also IBM equipment.

Computers: role in bibliographic control, 10.

Consultants: for library automation project, 94–95, 98–99.

Contracts: for turnkey systems, 24–34 passim; cancellation of, 40; in WLN, 55.

Conversion of catalog records to machine-readable form: use of mini-MARC format, 7; at U. of Illinois Undergraduate Library, 41, 45, 48; problems with, 92–93, 99. See also Bibliographic data.

Cost effectiveness: of manual systems, 6; effect of automation on, 6.

Cost estimates, 39. See also Procurement of automated systems.

Costs: of computers, 6; of personnel, 6; of card catalog, 10; of development of automated system, 45, 47; of conversion of catalog records to machine-readable form, 92–93.

Data transmission, 42. See also Telecommunication cable.

DEC-1077, 77, 81.

Design of systems: and scheduling, 8; flaws in, 48.

Designers of automated systems: relationship with librarians, 5.

Development of automated systems: and research, 20–22; and reporting of failures, 21–22.

Dewey Decimal Classification system: conversion to Library of Congress system, 91–101.

Eastern Illinois University Library, 40.

Failures in library automation: reasons for, 4–14; lack of reporting on, 16–

Programming: and scheduling, 8. *See also* Software.
Public libraries in India, 75–76.

Quality control of automated records, 51–52.

Reclassification: from Dewey Decimal to Library of Congress system, 91–101.
Research: and development, 20–21; and discovery of fundamental laws, 20–21.
Richard Abel Company, 99.

Scheduling: problems of, 8, 9.
Software: problems in development in Japan, 13; in WLN, 58–59; problems with, in India, 81. *See also* Programming.
Special libraries in India, 76.
Storage capacity: of computers, in India, 81.
Students of library automation. *See* Library school students.

TCAM, 43.
Teaching library automation: goals of course, 67–68.
Technicians: relationship of, with librarians, 5.
Technology: as master of library automation, 5, 14; false hope in, 6; in libraries, 9.
Telecommunication cable, 42, 46, 49.
Thomas, Lewis: quoted, 12–13.
3M Corporation, 99.
Training in library automation, 84–85.
Turnkey circulation systems. *See* Circulation systems.

Union catalogs: dysfunction of, 13–14.
University of Illinois Undergraduate Library: circulation system, 35–49.
University of Illinois Graduate School of Library Science, 74.
UTLAS, 60–65.

Washington Library Commission, 55.
Washington State Data Processing Authority, 52, 54, 55.
Washington University School of Medicine Libary, 16.
WLN, 50–59.